FOOD PROCESSORS
PROPERLY EXPLAINED

FOOD PROCESSORS PROPERLY EXPLAINED

WITH RECIPES

Dianne Page

RIGHT WAY

CONTENTS

INTRODUCTION

As my family and friends will testify, I love cooking – as long as I don't get my hands dirty. Not for me the delights of getting to grips, literally, with bread dough, stuffings or pastry; not for me the arm-aching creaming of cakes, nor the manicure-wrecking grating of cheese and breadcrumbs.

The arrival of food processors opened up new culinary horizons for me. I was amazed at their versatility, power and speed. They turned pastry-making from a chore into an easy two-minute operation, and bread-making from a complex rite into a fool-proof success every time.

This didn't happen overnight, though, but new techniques soon were learnt and traditional methods adapted. I hope that my experience, now included in this book, will help if you are contemplating buying a food processor, have recently acquired one, or feel you could achieve more with the one you already own.

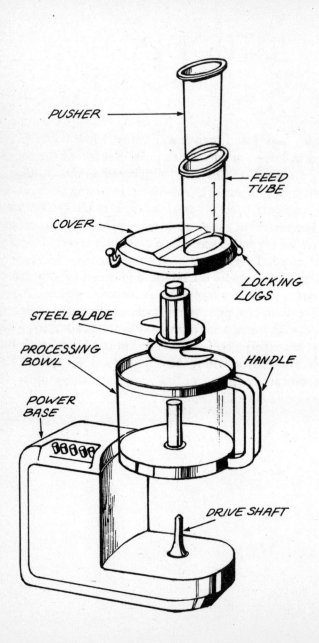

PUSHER

FEED
TUBE

COVER

LOCKING
LUGS

STEEL BLADE

PROCESSING
BOWL

HANDLE

POWER
BASE

DRIVE SHAFT

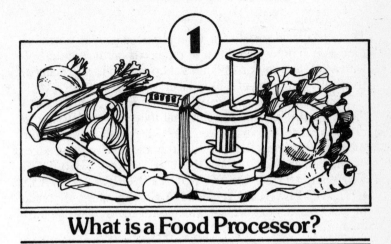

What is a Food Processor?

A good food processor can do much of the work of liquidisers and food mixers. All the food is processed in one bowl, whether chopped, mixed, puréed, sliced or grated, using a few attachments which are simple to fit and no problem to store. In addition, you can choose a more sophisticated model which may well include accessories that extend the usage of your food processor. Some models have a separate blender goblet, citrus press, herb and spice mill or juice extractor. As all models vary from brand to brand, please read carefully your manufacturer's handbook so that you understand how your food processor should be used.

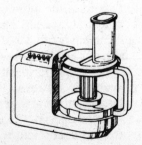

THE BOWL

The bowl is made of a tough, clear plastic so you can watch the food as it is processed. Most of the bowls on the market will withstand the addition of liquids at boiling point and many of them may be washed in a dishwasher.

The lid of the bowl is also of clear plastic and incorporates a feed tube through which additional food may be introduced during a processing operation. A plastic pusher fits within the tube and this keeps fingers away from the sharp cutting edges of the attachments. NEVER PUSH FOOD THROUGH THE FEED TUBE USING YOUR FINGERS – ALWAYS USE THE PUSHER PROVIDED. Some pushers are made of clear plastic and are calibrated with metric and imperial quantities for use as a handy measuring cup.

THE MOTOR

The bowl sits on a central spindle which creates the drive for the attachments. The powerful motor is situated beside the bowl in most food processors (see front cover), but in a couple of cases the bowl sits on top of the motor, so taking up slightly less space on the work top. The motors vary in power from model to model, and some processors are belt driven while others are driven by an induction motor.

The speed of the motor is the main difference between food processors, and as the number of speeds provided affects the price, you need to appreciate the benefits of multi-speed. The basic models generally operate at only one speed which equates with the fastest speed of the more expensive processors providing a choice of up to 12 speeds. The more advanced models detect which attachment is fitted and adjust the speed automatically to suit the task. The recipes which follow have all been tested on a very basic single speed processor and I found the results very acceptable, however, the advantages of multi-speed cannot be denied and the slower speeds allow you to whisk egg whites (with the special attachment) and mix cakes and yeasted mixtures more satisfactorily.

On occasions it is necessary to chop or blend additional food using a pulsing action, a short burst of power which allows you to control the degree of processing. The more sophisticated models are fitted with a pulse button, but with the basic processors you need to do this manually by switching the motor on and off (at the appliance, not at the wall switch). A pulse button is a useful facility as it is so easy to over-process, especially when chopping.

THE ATTACHMENTS

Steel Blade

The universal attachment of all food processors is the steel blade, a very sharp double-bladed knife which sits on the drive spindle and whizzes around at amazing speed to chop, mix, blend and purée. Most recipes require the steel blade for all or part of the operation and in my instructions "processing" means the use of the steel blade.

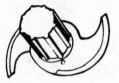

A Steel Blade

Take care always to handle this attachment by its plastic stem to avoid cutting yourself. It is best to leave the steel blade fitted onto the drive spindle when the processor isn't in use as storage elsewhere could lead to accidents and blunting of the cutting edges. Some manufacturers provide useful plastic sleeves to protect the blades.

Plastic Blade

Not standard on all processors, the plastic blade resembles the steel blade but, instead of two sharp cutting knives, the blunt plastic allows you to mix in without chopping and is recommended for use with bread, pastry and cake mixes. Useful but not essential.

Dough Hook
For bread it is preferable to use the dough hook with its bent prongs designed to knead the mixture rather than just blend it.

Slicing Disc
All models are provided with a slicing disc which fits onto the drive spindle, positioning the cutting disc close to the lid. Food is pushed through the feed tube and as the disc rotates at high speed, the food is sliced and falls into the bottom of the bowl.

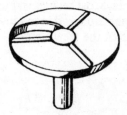

A Slicing Disc

The earlier discs had a fixed stem which fitted over the drive spindle. This presented a minor storage problem, soon overcome though by the provision of an ingenious wall rack into which the various discs could be slotted. Some of the later models provide interchangeable discs which can be clipped onto a single plastic stem or disc carrier, a much neater solution.

Shredding/Grating Disc
As with the slicing disc, the shredding/grating disc is a standard accessory and operates in exactly the same way. One manufacturer has incorporated both slicing and shredding in one disc and you simply reverse the blade on the disc carrier

A Shredding/Grating Disc

for whichever operation is required. On another model the disc can be reversed to give coarse shredding on one side and fine grating on the other. Some manufacturers offer a wider range of grating coarseness, from a very fine Parmesan grater to a coarser shredder to produce juliennes or thicker strips of vegetables.

Chipper Disc

The chipper disc is standard on only a few models and is an optional extra on some but not all. It operates like the other discs but tends to produce Continental size chips, not the fat ones favoured by home-made chip connoisseurs. A useful addition if the family are great chip eaters.

Whisk

In the past the greatest criticism of food processors was their inability to whisk egg whites and whip cream. In fact it is possible to whip cream using the steel blade, but some manufacturers have brought out attachments to whip cream

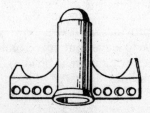

A Whisk

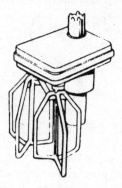

A Whisk with Traditional Beaters

and/or whisk egg whites.

In one case this is a plastic paddle with holes to incorporate air into the egg whites. In another case a fluted disk is fitted to the drive spindle and produces good results. A couple of models have an attachment with two traditional beaters which fit into a gearing head which in turn sits on the drive spindle. As the gearing head rotates around the bowl, the two beaters whisk the contents until egg whites are light and frothy or cream is whipped.

One food processor has a second bowl which fits within the first. It incorporates a single head rotating whisk which revolves around the bowl to whisk egg whites and whip cream. Once prepared, the second bowl can be removed and put aside, or stored in the fridge until needed.

Dough Kit
One manufacturer provides an extra bowl with a special domed lid to allow you to leave your mixed bread to rise in the same bowl. This frees your normal bowl and lid for other processing in the meantime.

Citrus Press
If you have access to lots of citrus fruit to make fruit drinks,

this is a useful attachment, otherwise a manual press is more than adequate for the small number you need to press in everyday cookery.

Juice Extractor
This attachment enables you to obtain the juice of fruit and vegetables. A drum and strainer basket fit into the standard bowl but have a special cover and pusher.

Using your Food Processor

All food processors operate slightly differently, so always read your handbook before first use. They are all designed to provide maximum safety and many of them won't operate if not correctly assembled. The bowl fits onto the base and is rotated to lock into position. You then fit the steel blade or other attachment. Fitting the lid correctly ensures that the machine will operate; a major safety precaution to prevent fingers reaching the sharp blades while they are still moving. With most models the lid is rotated so that lugs on the lid and bowl lock together. At the same time a projecting lug passes through a slot into the motor base, and it is this which allows the machine to run. In some of the earlier models this was the only way to switch on the processor and the lid has to be rotated smartly to and fro to produce the pulsing action. With recent models this slot in the motor base is still a safety device but there is usually an on/off switch and/or a speed and pulse control.

Keep the pusher in the feed tube during processing. It is safer to do so and it prevents food flying up at you. For the same reason never remove the lid until the blades or disc have completely stopped.

If your machine has variable speeds use the slower one to

mince meat, chop onions and herbs, the middle speed for making cakes and yeasted mixtures, the fastest for puréeing, fine chopping, slicing, and shredding.

Advice on specific areas of cooking is given in the following recipes but there are some general guidelines which may be useful.

Fit the blade or whisk before adding the food.

Food to be chopped should be cut evenly, otherwise the smaller pieces will be over-processed before the larger ones are chopped.

Don't overfill the processor bowl. For one thing liquid will spill out of the lid or onto the drive spindle, for another, solid foods will be processed unevenly. Each bowl has its recommended maximum capacity for liquids, chopping and flour mixtures, so please check your handbook.

Scrape down the food. As food is processed it is flung outwards by the centrifugal force. To ensure a complete blend of ingredients, remove the lid and scrape the food from the sides to the middle, using the spatula provided.

Check liquid quantity. Food processing is so efficient that you may require slightly less liquid. Add it gradually through the feed tube and check progress.

Don't over-process. The blades rotate so fast it is easy to process food too long. It is far better to under-process, check and process for a further few seconds, especially when you are learning how to use your machine.

Remove the bowl before the food. Twist the bowl and remove it from the motor base before removing the disc or blade, and then the food. This prevents food trickling down the drive spindle.

Wash the bowl only when necessary. If ingredients are being processed separately but for use in the same recipe, it is generally unnecessary to wash the bowl and blade between operations.

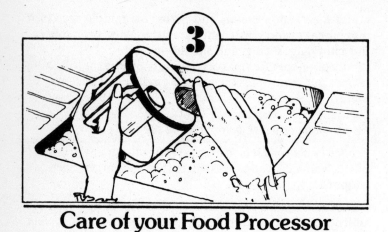

Care of your Food Processor

Always switch off and disconnect the appliance before cleaning. Clean the plastic casing of the motor base with a damp, not wet, cloth. The plastic bowl and lid should be washed in hot, soapy water, rinsed and dried. Check the manufacturer's handbook whether they may be washed in a dishwasher.

The blades and discs should be washed similarly but ensure that there is no food lodged in the grating holes. It may be necessary to use a bottle brush to clean up inside the stem of the blade; some models are poorly designed and have awkward food traps. I find the dishwasher ideal to get them really clean.

When not in use, secure the bowl and steel blade and fit the lid loosely with the pusher in position. This allows a slight airflow to prevent mustiness over a long period. Don't leave the lid locked into the motor base.

Recipe notes

Follow either metric or imperial measures for the recipes in this book as they are not interchangeable.

Size 3 eggs should be used except where otherwise stated.

Plain flour and granulated sugar are used unless otherwise stated.

Sets of spoon measures are available in both metric and imperial size to give accurate measurement of small quantities.

The following symbols indicate which attachments should be used in each recipe:

🔪 **Steel blade**
🥬 **Slicing disc**
🥕 **Grating disc**

Soups

A soup can be a delicate starter to a dinner party, a light lunch-time snack, or a hearty meal in itself; whichever, your food processor can help you concoct creamed soups of velvety smoothness and speed up the preparation of chunky vegetable soups.

Creamed soups
If a soup is to be blended after cooking, it makes sense to cut down on cooking time by chopping the vegetables small to begin with. If a number of vegetables are to be cooked together they may also be processed together, but take care not to overload the bowl.

Onions flavour most soups, so place the peeled and quartered onion(s) into the bowl fitted with the steel blade and process until finely chopped. Additional flavourings may be added through the feed tube, dropping them in chunks onto the turning blade.

For large quantities of the same vegetable, eg. carrot, cauliflower, beetroot or parsnips, use the grating or slicing disc.

When puréeing a soup it is important not to overload the bowl with liquid otherwise it will leak through the spindle or lid. One solution is to halve the cooking liquid and top it up before final re-heating, but I prefer to strain the liquid into a clean pan and spoon the solids from the sieve into the processor bowl. Take care to remove any bouquet garni or bay leaf first. Process until smooth, then transfer the purée into the liquid, scraping the sides of the bowl to capture every drop of flavouring. Stir while reheating and add milk, cream or yoghurt at this stage. Do not boil the soup after adding these unless it contains cornflour.

Chunky soups
To me chunky soups are simply those which are not puréed after cooking, and the food processor is a great help during preparation.

The vegetables should be cut into pieces that will sit easily on a soup spoon. For example, carrots are preferably chopped rather than sliced, except when used in what are called main course soups. Celery looks more attractive sliced rather than chopped, but the broader outer sticks should be halved lengthways to produce neater slices. When adding cabbage to a soup use the slicing disc, pressing down lightly on the pusher to ensure finely shredded strips.

Both puréed and chunky soups can be cooked even more quickly in a pressure cooker; recipes such as Tomato, Orange and Lentil, and Continental Pea Soup cook in a fraction of the time of conventional cooking.

CREAM OF WATERCRESS SOUP *Serves 4–6*

1 onion, peeled and quartered
2—3 cloves of garlic (*optional*)
25g (1 oz) butter
1 bunch of watercress
550ml (1 pint) chicken stock
salt and pepper
300ml (½ pint) milk
1 tbsp cornflour

Put the onion and garlic into the bowl and process until finely chopped. Melt the butter in a medium sized pan and gently fry the onion and garlic until softened but not browned. Remove any discoloured leaves from the watercress and put the well-washed bunch of leaves and stems into the pan. Add the stock and seasoning, bring to the boil then simmer gently for about 20 minutes until cooked through. Remove from the heat and strain the liquid into a clean pan. Transfer the watercress from the sieve to the processor bowl and process until finely chopped. Add the cornflour and a little of the milk. Process until well blended. Stir this into the soup with the remaining milk and bring to the boil over a medium heat, stirring until thickened. Simmer for a couple of minutes before serving.

CREAM OF CAULIFLOWER ♀ ⚓   *Serves 4–6*

1 head of cauliflower, separated into florets
550ml (1 pint) vegetable stock
15ml (1 tbsp) cornflour
300ml (½ pint) milk
salt and pepper
croûtons to garnish

Use the slicing disc to slice the cauliflower florets. Put the sliced cauliflower into a large saucepan and add the stock. Cook until softened. Fit the steel blade. Strain the cooking liquid into a clean pan and process the cauliflower until puréed. Add the cornflour and milk and process until well blended. Stir into the liquid and bring to the boil over a medium heat, stirring continuously. Simmer for a few minutes, season and serve sprinkled with hot croûtons.

CELERY SOUP ♀ ⚓   *Serves 4–6*

1 head of celery, trimmed and washed
25g (1 oz) butter
550ml (1 pint) chicken stock
bouquet garni
2 tsp cornflour
up to 300ml (½ pint) milk
salt and pepper

Chop the celery using the slicing disc. Melt the butter in a large saucepan and gently sauté the celery for 5 minutes. Add the stock and bouquet garni, bring to the boil and simmer for 30 minutes until the celery is softened. Discard the bouquet garni. Strain the liquid into a measuring jug. Fit the steel blade and purée the cooked celery. Add the cornflour and process to blend. Add sufficient milk to the liquid to make 550ml (1 pint) and pour into a clean saucepan. Stir the purée into the pan and bring to the boil, stirring continuously. Simmer for a couple of minutes and season the thickened soup.

CARROT AND SWEETCORN SOUP ♀ ⚓

1 onion, peeled and quartered   *Serves 4–6*
450g (1 lb) carrots, peeled
225g (8 oz) sweetcorn (tinned or frozen)

25g (1 oz) butter
850ml (1½ pints) chicken or vegetable stock
salt and pepper
1 tbsp cornflour
single cream *(optional)*

Fit the grating disc and grate the onion and carrots. Heat the butter in a large saucepan and stir in all the vegetables until completely coated. Cook covered over a gentle heat for 2-3 minutes. Add the stock and seasoning and bring to the boil. Simmer for 45 minutes until softened. Strain the liquid into a clean saucepan and put the cooked vegetables into the bowl, now fitted with the steel blade. Add the cornflour and process until well blended. Stir the purée into the liquid, bring to the boil, stirring continuously, season and serve, with a swirl of cream, if wished.

TOMATO, ORANGE AND LENTIL SOUP ✌

Serves 4–6

2 oranges
1 onion, peeled and quartered
450g (1 lb) tomatoes, skinned and de-seeded
850ml (1½ pints) chicken or vegetable stock
2 tablespoons tomato purée
salt and pepper
225g (8 oz) orange lentils
bouquet garni
150ml (¼ pint) single cream

Finely chop the zest of 1 orange (see page 125). Put the onion into the bowl and process until roughly chopped. Add the tomatoes and process until pulped. Squeeze the juice from the two oranges and put into a large saucepan with all the remaining ingredients, except the cream. Bring to the boil and simmer for 2-3 hours until the lentils are softened. Remove the bouquet garni and strain the liquid into a clean pan or bowl. Purée the remaining residue until velvety smooth. Stir this purée into the liquid and adjust seasoning if necessary. When cold stir in the cream. Serve chilled and garnish with finely chopped parsley.

BEETROOT SOUP ☼ ❦   *Serves 4–6*

450g (1 lb) raw beetroot
juice of 2 oranges
1 litre (2 pints) chicken stock
2 tsp salt
black pepper
soured cream
chopped fresh parsley

Peel the beetroot and cut into chunks to fit the feed tube. Use the
grating disc to grate the beetroot. As this is a particularly hard root,
don't press too hard and allow the pieces to tumble slightly in the
feed tube, grating on all faces. Transfer to a large saucepan. Add
the orange juice, chicken stock and seasoning, bring to the boil and
simmer on a gentle heat for an hour. Strain the liquid into a clean
pan. Fit the steel blade and turn the beetroot into the bowl. Process
until smooth and stir into the liquid. Adjust seasoning and reheat.
Serve with a swirl of soured cream and sprinkled with parsley.

VICHYSSOISE ❧ ❦   *Serves 4–6*

700g (1½ lb) leeks *(trimmed weight)*
1 small potato, peeled
25g (1 oz) butter
850ml (1½ pints) chicken stock
salt
single cream or yoghurt
finely chopped fresh chives

Traditionally only the white leaves of the leek should be used to
give the characteristic white appearance of this soup, but a few light
green leaves give this soup an attractive colour. Wash the leeks with
care to remove all soil and slice using the slicing disc. Melt the
butter in a large saucepan and stir in the sliced leeks until coated
with the butter. Leave to cook on a low heat. Slice the potato and
add to the leeks. Add the stock and salt and simmer for 20-30
minutes until softened. Strain the liquid into a clean pan. Fit the
steel blade and process the leeks and potatoes until puréed. Stir
into the liquid, taste, and adjust the seasoning. If to be served cold,
stir in single cream or yoghurt and chill for a couple of hours before
serving. Alternatively, reheat the soup and stir in the cream just
before serving. Sprinkle either version with the chives.

SPICY TOMATO SOUP ✍ *Serves 4–6*

1kg (2 lb) ripe tomatoes
1 tbsp olive oil
2 onions, peeled and quartered
2 cloves garlic
2 tbsp tomato purée
½ tsp chilli sauce
1 tsp salt
1 tbsp lemon juice
plain yoghurt (*optional*)

Prick the tomatoes and plunge into a pan or bowl of boiling water for 30 seconds. Remove and plunge into cold water for a minute. The skins may then be removed easily. Halve the tomatoes, cutting away the tough stalk end. Process the onions and garlic until finely chopped. Heat the oil in a large flame-proof casserole or saucepan and gently fry the onions until softened but not browned. Put the tomatoes and remaining ingredients into the processor bowl and process until completely puréed. Pour over the onions, bring to the boil then simmer covered for half an hour. Adjust seasoning if necessary and serve hot or cold with a swirl of yoghurt if wished.

PARSNIP & CURRY SOUP ✍ ✍ *Serves 4–6*

1 onion, peeled and quartered
25g (1 oz) butter
700g (1½ lb) parsnips, peeled
1 cooking apple, peeled and cored
1 tbsp curry powder
850ml (1½ pints) chicken stock
salt
plain yoghurt (*optional*)

Use the slicing disc to slice the onion. Heat the butter in a large saucepan and fry the onion until softened but not browned. Slice the parsnips and apple together and stir into the saucepan. Add the curry powder, stock and salt. Bring to the boil and simmer for about 45 minutes. Strain the liquid into a clean pan and fit the steel blade. Purée the parsnip mixture and stir into the liquid. Adjust seasoning and re-heat. Serve in individual bowls with a swirl of yoghurt.

CONTINENTAL PEA SOUP 🍷 ⚓   *Serves 4–6*

225g (8 oz) dried split peas
550ml (1 pint) boiling water
1 onion, peeled and quartered
3 sticks of celery
25g (1 oz) butter
1 litre (2 pints) chicken stock
150g (6 oz) garlic sausage
½ tsp sage
salt and pepper

Pour boiling water over the peas, cover and soak overnight. Next day use the slicing disc to slice the onion and celery. Fry in the butter in a large saucepan. Do not allow to brown. Drain the peas and add to the saucepan. Add the stock and bring to the boil. After 10 minutes boiling remove any scum, if necessary. Put the garlic sausage through the slicer and add to the soup. Add the herbs and simmer for 2-3 hours until softened. Strain the liquid into a clean pan. Fit the steel blade and process the peas and sausage until puréed. Stir into the liquid, season and reheat for serving. Garnish with croûtons.

FARMHOUSE VEGETABLE SOUP 🌿 ⚓
Serves 4–6

3 onions, peeled and quartered
25g (1 oz) butter
5 carrots
3 parsnips
3 potatoes
850ml (1½ pints) chicken stock
397g (14 oz) can tomatoes
1 tbsp cornflour
2 tbsp tomato purée
salt and pepper
bay leaf

Use the grating disc to grate the onions. Melt the butter in a large saucepan and fry the onions over a gentle heat until softened but not browned. Meanwhile grate the carrots, parsnips and potatoes. Stir into the saucepan and pour over the stock. Fit the steel blade and put into the bowl the contents of the can of tomatoes, the cornflour, tomato purée, salt and pepper. Process until blended and add to the saucepan with the bay leaf. Bring to the boil, stirring, and simmer for an hour. Remove the bay leaf and serve with freshly chopped chives.

MINESTRONE SOUP ☙ 🌿 🌿 ☙   *Serves 4–6*

1 onion quartered
1-2 cloves garlic
1 green pepper, de-seeded and quartered
1 tbsp olive oil
4 sticks celery
2 carrots
227g (8 oz) can of tomatoes
4 tbsp tomato purée
850ml (1½ pints) chicken stock
½ tsp oregano
salt and black pepper
¼ shredded cabbage
50g (2 oz) macaroni
grated parmesan cheese

Process the onion, garlic and pepper until coarsely chopped. Heat the oil in a large, heavy based saucepan and gently fry the onion, garlic and pepper until softened but not browned. Fit the slicing disc and slice the celery. Transfer to the pan. Shred the cabbage and retain it to one side. Fit the grating disc and grate the carrot. Transfer to the pan. Fit the steel blade and add the can of tomatoes and the tomato purée. Process until blended then add to the pan. Add stock, seasoning and oregano, bring to the boil and simmer for 30 minutes. Add the cabbage and macaroni and cook for a further 30 minutes. Serve sprinkled with parmesan cheese and accompanied by hot crusty bread.

FRENCH ONION SOUP 🌿 🌿   *Serves 4–6*

450g (1 lb) onion
1-2 cloves garlic
50g (2 oz) butter
850ml (1½ pints) beef stock
salt and pepper
4-6 slices of French bread
50g (2 oz) cheddar cheese

Fit the slicing disc and slice the onions and garlic. Heat the butter in a large saucepan and fry both until golden brown. Stir in the beef stock and bring to the boil, simmering for 30 minutes. Fit the grating disc and grate the cheese. When the soup is cooked, season to taste and ladle into soup bowls. Sprinkle the bread with cheese, float the bread on the soup and stand under a hot grill until the cheese is bubbling. Serve at once.

GAZPACHO &   *Serves 4-6*

1 onion, quartered
2 cloves garlic
1 green pepper, de-seeded and quartered
1 red pepper, de-seeded and quartered
450g (1 lb) tomatoes, skinned and de-seeded
300ml ($\frac{1}{2}$ pint) olive oil
150ml ($\frac{1}{4}$ pint) wine vinegar
$\frac{1}{2}$ cucumber, washed
salt and pepper
ice cubes
stuffed olives to garnish

Process the onion and garlic until coarsely chopped. Add the green and red pepper and process until finely chopped. Add the tomatoes, olive oil and wine vinegar and process until well blended. Pour into a large chilled serving bowl. Fit the grating disc and grate the unpeeled cucumber. Stir into the soup, season to taste, chill and serve with icecubes floating in the bowl. Serve sliced stuffed olives as an accompaniment.

Pâtés, Terrines and Spreads

Use the power and speed of the steel blade to reduce cooked and uncooked meat, fish and poultry to a delightful range of pâtés, terrines and spreads. Take care though not to over-process. Some pâtés are intended to be coarse in texture so process in short bursts and frequently check the appearance of the chopped ingredients.

Anyone who has to make sandwiches regularly knows how difficult it is to find something a bit different from the usual cheese, egg or cold meat fillings. By using the food processor these same basic, inexpensive ingredients can be transformed into exciting spreads for more satisfying lunch-time snacks.

The same spreads provide excellent fillings for toasted sandwiches, whether made under the grill or in an electric sandwich toaster. For more interesting tea-time or supper snacks, spread the mixtures thickly on halved scones (p. 117) or on individual circles of shortbread (p. 119).

CHICKEN LIVER PÂTÉ 🍳   *Serves 6–8*

1 onion, quartered
clove garlic *(optional)*
25g (1 oz) butter
450g (1 lb) chicken livers
salt
freshly ground black pepper
1 egg
2 tbsp sherry

Process the onion and garlic until finely chopped. Melt the butter in a frypan and fry the onion and garlic gently until softened but not browned. Remove any skin or gall from the livers and add the livers to the frypan. Fry briefly until browned on all sides, then transfer to the bowl and add all the remaining ingredients. Process until smoothly blended. Pour into a greased 500ml (1 pint) soufflé dish and cover with foil. Stand in a baking tin and pour into the tin sufficient boiling water to come half-way up the dish. Cook in the middle of the oven (170°C, 325°F, Gas Mark 3) for about 1 hour. Remove from the oven and place a weight over the pâté to compress it. Serve when cold.

COUNTRY PORK PÂTÉ ✍   *Serves 6–8*

1 onion, peeled and quartered
1-2 cloves garlic (*optional*)
1kg (2 lb) belly pork
225g (8 oz) sausagemeat
salt
good pinch of freshly grated nutmeg
¼ tsp dried sage
2 tbsp cranberry sauce
1 egg
6 slices of streaky bacon, de-rinded

Put the onion and garlic into the bowl and process until roughly chopped. Remove the rind and bones from the belly pork and cut into 2.5cm (1 in) pieces. Put half the meat into the bowl and process until finely chopped. Remove the contents of the bowl and keep on one side. Process the remaining meat until finely chopped, then add the sausagemeat. Process until well mixed. Add the salt, nutmeg, sage, cranberry sauce and egg and process to mix. Add the first batch of meat and process until all is well blended. Grease a large loaf tin. With the back of a knife stretch the bacon thinly on a chopping board. Line the loaf tin with the bacon, laying it across the tin with the ends spilling over the side. Spoon the mixture into the tin and smooth it level. Fold the bacon ends over the pâté. Cover with foil and stand in a roasting tin with hot water reaching half-way up the side of the loaf tin. Cook in this water bath for 2 hours at 170°C, 325°F, Gas Mark 3. Test with a skewer to ensure the pâté is cooked. Remove the tin and the foil. Make a pad from the folded foil, cover the top of the pâté with this and leave to cool with a weight pressing down on the pad. When cold turn out the pâté and serve with crusty French bread.

GAME PÂTÉ &   *Serves 6–8*

2 pigeons, plucked and cleaned
350g (12 oz) boned rabbit, cubed
550ml (1 pint) chicken stock
bay leaf
½ tsp coriander seed
1 onion, peeled and quartered
100g (4 oz) streaky bacon, de-rinded
225g (8 oz) turkey livers
1 egg
1 tsp salt
black pepper
pinch of tarragon
2 tbsp sherry

Use a sharp knife to cut the breasts from the pigeons. Put the pigeon carcasses and the rabbit into a saucepan with the stock and bay leaf. Use the steel blade to crush the coriander seed and add this to the pan. Bring to the boil and simmer for 20 minutes. Cut the pigeon breasts into large cubes, put into the bowl and process briefly until roughly chopped. Remove from the bowl. Put the onion into the bowl and chop coarsely. Cut the bacon into smaller pieces, add to the bowl and process until finely chopped. Add all the remaining uncooked ingredients and process until smooth. Remove this mixture and rinse out the bowl and steel blade. Using a slotted spoon transfer the cooked rabbit into the bowl. Continue cooking the pigeon carcasses to make a game stock for soups or casseroles. Briefly process the rabbit to form small pea-sized pieces. Grease a large loaf tin (of the pressed, not folded construction) and pour in half the liver mixture. Sprinkle over a layer of the chopped rabbit and then a layer of the chopped pigeon breasts. Finally pour over the remaining liver mixture. Cover with aluminium foil and stand in a roasting tin with sufficient water to reach about 2.5cm (1 in) up the side of the loaf tin. Put this water bath into the centre of a medium oven, 170°C, 325°F, Gas Mark 3, and cook for 2 hours. When cooked (test with a skewer), remove from the oven and leave to cool under a weight as described in Country Pork Pâté. Turn out and serve cold, glazed with redcurrant jelly and decorated with bay leaves, or serve hot or cold en croûte, see next recipe.

PÂTÉ EN CROÛTE

A coarse pâté such as Game Pâté or Country Pork Pâté may be encased in pastry, baked and served hot or cold. Make 225g (8 oz) of shortcrust pastry (p. 102) and roll out to form a rectangle sufficient to wrap up the pâté. Stand the cold pâté on the pastry and neatly fold over the pastry to form a parcel. Moisten the edges of the pastry to ensure a good seal. Place on a greased baking tray, with the pastry seam underneath, decorate with leaf shapes cut from the remaining pastry, and brush with beaten egg or milk. Bake for 35 minutes at 220°C, 425°F, Gas Mark 7, until golden brown. Use a fish slice to transfer the pâté carefully to a serving dish.

TUNA & AVOCADO TERRINE   *Serves 4*

425ml (¾ pint) milk
couple of sprigs of parsley
1 small onion, peeled
1 sachet gelatine
3 tbsp water
25g (1 oz) butter
1 tbsp cornflour
salt and white pepper
212g (7½ oz) can of tuna in oil
12 stuffed olives
1 ripe avocado pear

Put the parsley, onion, butter, cornflour and milk into the bowl and process until the parsley and onion are finely chopped. Pour into a saucepan and bring to the boil, stirring until thickened to make a white sauce. Simmer for a further 3 minutes on the lowest possible heat. Meanwhile put the water into a cup and sprinkle over the gelatine. Stand the cup in a pan of boiling water and stir until dissolved. Without rinsing the bowl chop the drained tuna, add eight of the olives and process until roughly chopped. Pour in the slightly cooled white sauce and dissolved gelatine and process with a pulse action to combine the ingredients. Grease a small loaf tin and pour one third of the mixture over the base. Halve the avocado, remove the stone and skin. Slice the avocado thinly crosswise forming crescent shapes. Arrange half the slices, slightly overlapping, down the length of the tin, then cover with the second third of the sauce. Repeat with the remaining avocado and sauce.

Leave to set in the refrigerator for a few hours. To serve, dip the tin in a bowl of hot water, and if necessary loosen the edges with a knife and turn out. Garnish with slices of stuffed olive and serve with crusty French bread.

SUMMER VEGETABLE TERRINE 🍸 🐚

75g (3 oz) young carrots, peeled
100g (4 oz) sweetcorn, frozen or canned
175g (6 oz) cut French beans, fresh or frozen
25g (1 oz) butter
25g (1 oz) cornflour
850ml (1½ pints) milk
chicken stock cube
bunch of fresh parsley
salt and pepper
1 sachet of gelatine
3 tbsp water

Serves 6–8

Using the slicing disc slice the carrots thickly and cook in a pan of boiling salted water for 5 minutes. Drain, cover in cold water, drain again and keep to one side (this is called "refreshing"). If the sweetcorn is tinned, simply drain away the liquid, otherwise cook in boiling water for 5 minutes. Refresh as with the carrots and keep separately on one side. If the beans are fresh, slice thickly using the slicing disc. Cook the fresh or frozen cut beans for 5 minutes and refresh as before. Keep separately on one side.

Fit the steel blade and finely chop the bunch of parsley. Add the butter, cornflour, chicken stock cube and 300ml (½ pint) of the milk. Process until well blended, pour into a pan with the remaining milk and bring to the boil, stirring continuously until thickened. Season to taste. Put the water into a cup and sprinkle over the gelatine. Stand the cup in a saucepan of simmering water and stir until dissolved. Stir into the slightly cooled sauce, blending thoroughly.

Grease a large loaf tin or two small tins. Spoon a thin layer of mixture over the bottom of the tin(s). Take care not to use too much at this stage – it has to last another three layers. Refrigerate to set. On this set sauce carefully arrange a layer of the beans, running lengthwise for neater cutting of slices. Leave a slight margin for the next layer of sauce to seep down the sides. Spoon over the second layer of sauce and leave to set. Neatly arrange a layer of carrot slices over the sauce. Spoon over sufficient mixture to cover and leave to set. Stir the sweetcorn into the remaining sauce and spoon over to form the top (or bottom when turned out) layer. Leave to set in the refrigerator. To serve, dip the tin briefly in a bowl of hot water and turn out onto a serving dish. Garnish with overlapping slices of cucumber and lemon.

VEGETARIAN SUPPER LOAF   *Serves 6*

225g (8 oz) mature cheddar cheese
bunch of fresh parsley
50g (2 oz) rye crisp bread, broken into pieces
1 green pepper, de-seeded and quartered
1 onion, peeled and quartered
25g (1 oz) butter
8 eggs
198g (7 oz) can of sweetcorn and mixed peppers
salt and black pepper

Cut the cheese into chunks and process until finely chopped. Remove from the bowl. Process the parsley with the crispbread until finely chopped. Remove from the bowl. Process the pepper and onion until finely chopped and fry in the butter until softened. Process the eggs in the bowl until well blended and add the cheese, parsley, crispbread, pepper and onion and all remaining ingredients. Process with short pulses to ensure mixture is well blended. Grease a large loaf tin and line the base with greased greaseproof paper. Pour the mixture into the tin and bake at 180°C, 350°F, Gas Mark 4, for 1-1¼ hours or until just set. Allow to cool then turn out. Serve with salad.

CHEESY CASHEW ROLL   *Serves 4–6*

50g (2 oz) spring onions *(including the green stem)*
4 hard boiled eggs, halved
225g (8 oz) cream cheese
salt and black pepper
pinch of cayenne pepper
100g (4 oz) salted cashews

Process the spring onions until finely chopped. Add the hard boiled eggs and process briefly until coarsely chopped. Add the cream cheese and seasoning and process until well blended. Remove from the bowl and form into a roll. Wrap in foil and chill for 1-2 hours. Meanwhile wash the bowl and process the nuts until finely chopped. Roll the cheesy roll in the nuts and serve sliced as a starter or as a snack with cheese biscuits.

SMOKED SALMON POTS   *Serves 4–6*

This is quite rich but need not be expensive if you ask for smoked salmon off-cuts from your delicatessen.

175g (6 oz) smoked salmon
1 red pepper, de-seeded and quartered
350g (12 oz) cream cheese
2 tbsp yoghurt
cayenne pepper
black pepper

Put the roughly chopped salmon and red pepper into the bowl and process until finely chopped. Add all the remaining ingredients and process until smoothly blended. Serve in individual ramekin dishes, garnished with slice of lemon, accompanied by hot toast or pitta bread.

SMOKED MACKEREL PÂTÉ   *Serves 8*

450g (1 lb) smoked mackerel
225g (8 oz) cream cheese
6 tsp lemon juice
4 tsp creamed horseradish
lemon wedges and cucumber slices to garnish

Remove bones and skin from the fish. Put all ingredients into the bowl and process until completely blended. Spoon into a large loaf tin and refrigerate until set. Unmould and garnish with the lemon and cucumber.

POTTED CHICKEN   *Serves 4*

3 rashers of lean bacon, de-rinded
225g (8 oz) cooked chicken
pinch of ground mace
dash of Worcestershire sauce
50g (2 oz) softened butter
3 tbsp single cream
salt and pepper
50g (2 oz) melted butter

Grill the bacon until crisp. Process in the bowl until finely chopped. Add the chicken and process until finely chopped. Add all remaining ingredients except the melted butter and process until smoothly blended. Adjust seasoning if necessary and pack into individual ramekin dishes. Pour the melted butter over, and chill before serving garnished with parsley and accompanied by hot toast.

SANDWICH SPREADS

Each of the following is sufficient for 4 rounds of bread, i.e. 2 rounds of sandwiches.

NUTTY CHEESE SPREAD ✍

2 small or 1 large spring onion
100g (4 oz) Red Leicester cheese
10g ($\frac{1}{2}$ oz) walnut halves
3 tbsp mayonnaise
salt and pepper

Process the onion until roughly chopped. Add cubes of the cheese and process until finely chopped. Add the walnut halves and mayonnaise and process until the walnuts are roughly chopped and the spread is well blended. Adjust seasoning if necessary.

SPICY EGG FILLING ✍

3 hardboiled eggs, halved
1 tbsp mango pickle
2 tbsp mayonnaise
salt and pepper
10g ($\frac{1}{2}$ oz) sultanas

Process the eggs until roughly chopped. Add all remaining ingredients except the sultanas and process until well blended. Add the sultanas and mix in with a brief pulsing action.

TUNA TOMATO TREAT ✍

212g ($7\frac{1}{2}$ oz) can of tuna, drained and flaked
1 large gherkin, halved
4 tsp tomato purée
$\frac{1}{2}$ tsp lemon juice
salt and pepper

Put all the ingredients into the bowl and process until well blended.

ALL FRUITS SPREAD &

25g (1 oz) hazelnuts
1 ripe banana
1 sharp eating apple, (*e.g. Granny Smith's***) peeled and cored**
1 tsp apricot jam

Process the nuts until roughly chopped. Add the banana in chunks with the apple and apricot jam and process until the fruit is chopped.

Sauces and Dips

SAUCES

Sauces are intended to complement a meal, whether as an accompaniment to meat, fish, salads or puddings. The speed and simplicity of the food processor removes the mystique of sauce making, from the basic white sauce to delicately flavoured mayonnaise and hollandaise sauce.

Certainly in the case of the quick white sauce (p. 41) you remove any risk of lumps and reduce the time spent standing watchfully over the stove. And anyone who hasn't had the courage to make their own mayonnaise for fear of it curdling, can take heart, because even in the unlikely event of it happening with a food processor, disaster can be averted by following the tips on page 40.

DIPS

Whether served as a refreshing appetiser with crudités, or as an easy-to-eat nibble at a party, a dip is easily prepared and can be as exotic or as simple as you like.

The basis of most dips is cream cheese, mayonnaise, yoghurt or puréed vegetable, depending on the richness or sharpness of your taste. To these can be added a variety of flavourings including drained canned fish, cheeses, nuts, salad vegetables such as spring onion or green pepper, drained, canned or fresh fruit, even packet soups. The flavourings are best finely chopped or puréed using the steel blade, before adding the basis of the dip and processing until well blended.

Crudités can be served as a starter and are crisp, uncooked vegetables such as cucumber, courgette, green and red pepper, cauliflower and carrot, cut into strips 7cm (3 in) long and about 2cm (½ in) thick. Arrange them attractively on a serving dish with a choice of two or three dips, preferably of contrasting colours, served in ramekin dishes or small pots.

For a party dip provide potato crisps (p. 123), cheese sticks or Italian bread sticks.

VINAIGRETTE DRESSING &

Make this quantity and store it in a screw-top bottle in the refrigerator and it will last a couple of weeks or so – depending on how many salads you have.

150ml (¼ pint) wine vinegar
75ml (⅛ pint) olive oil
2 tbsp French mustard
salt
freshly ground black pepper

Put all the ingredients into the food processor with the steel blade and process until well blended. Store as above and shake well before use.

Variations of the basic vinaigrette are simple and it is interesting to experiment. Instead of wine vinegar, substitute lemon juice, cider vinegar or a vinegar flavoured with tarragon or garlic. Experiment with different oils and the wide range of flavoured mustards now available. A dash of soy sauce will give a Chinese taste to a salad of crisp vegetables. And of course a garlic clove or sprig of your favourite herb chopped in the bowl first of all will enliven any vinaigrette dressing.

MAYONNAISE &

1 egg, size 3 (*add a second yolk for a thicker mayonnaise*)
salt and pepper
¼ tsp dry mustard
2 tbsp wine vinegar
300ml (½ pint) olive oil

Have all the ingredients at room temperature. Put the egg, seasonings and vinegar into the bowl and process briefly until well blended. Remove the plastic pusher and with the motor running pour the oil through the filling tube in a thin steady stream. If the mayonnaise should curdle during this stage, add a few more drops of vinegar and process before adding more oil. If this mixture is still curdled, pour it into a jug, wash and dry the bowl and steel blade, and start again with another egg yolk, gradually adding the curdled mixture and then the remaining oil. At this stage adjust the seasoning or add other flavourings.

Variations

WATERCRESS MAYONNAISE, delicious with cold chicken or ham. Wash a bunch of watercress, discard any discoloured leaves or woody stems. Shake dry, add to the mayonnaise in the bowl and process until finely chopped.

SAUCE MARIE ROSE added to prawns, shrimp or crab makes a tasty Seafood Cocktail. Add to the mayonnaise 2 tbsp tomato purée and 1 tbsp brandy.

CURRY MAYONNAISE may be spooned over cold chicken or hard-boiled eggs. Add ½ tsp curry powder and 10g (½ oz) flaked almonds.

HERB MAYONNAISE, a good accompaniment to cold meat or fish. Wash and dry a small bunch of parsley and chives, chopped in half, and add to the mayonnaise in the bowl. Process until finely chopped. If preferred substitute favourite herbs.

AIOLI *(Garlic Mayonnaise)*

Aioli also makes a delicious dip with crudités, served as a starter.

4 garlic cloves
2 egg yolks
150ml (¼ pint) olive oil
5ml (1 tsp) white wine vinegar
juice of one lemon (2 tbsp)
salt and pepper

Put the garlic into the bowl and process until finely chopped. Add the egg yolks and process briefly to blend. Add the oil in a thin, steady stream through the filling tube, with the motor running. The sauce should now have thickened and the vinegar and lemon juice should be added with the motor running. Season to taste.

HOLLANDAISE SAUCE 🍃
(serve with fish, steak or asparagus)

3 tbsp white wine vinegar
6 black peppercorns
½ bay leaf
1 blade of mace
3 egg yolks
100g (4 oz) softened butter
salt and white pepper

Boil the vinegar with the peppercorns, bay leaf and mace until reduced to 1 tbsp. Strain and cool. Melt the butter in a saucepan. Put the egg yolks into the bowl with the cooled vinegar and 1 tbsp of the butter and process until well blended. With the motor running slowly pour the melted butter through the feed tube in a steady trickle. Gradually the sauce will thicken. Add the seasoning and serve while still warm. Don't try to re-heat or it will curdle.

WHITE SAUCE 🍃

A white sauce may be used for coating, as for Cauliflower Cheese, or made thinner for pouring, as for Brandy Sauce.

For coating: 25g (1 oz) softened butter,
25g (1 oz) cornflour,
250ml (½ pint) milk
For pouring: 15g (½ oz) softened butter,
15g (½ oz) cornflour
250ml (½ pint) milk

The method for both types of sauce is the same: put all the ingredients into the bowl and process until well blended, then transfer to a heavy based milkpan, preferably non-stick. Bring to the boil, stirring continuously and cook for a further 2 minutes. Always use a medium heat with a white sauce as a fierce heat could burn the bottom of the sauce. If you do make a lumpy sauce, return it to the bowl for a quick whizz until smooth.

Variations
PARSLEY SAUCE
Wash and dry a small bunch of fresh parsley. Remove the thicker stems and process in the bowl until finely chopped. Add the remaining ingredients for the White Sauce and proceed as above.

CHEESE SAUCE
Put 50g (2 oz) hard cheese, cubed, into the bowl and process until finely chopped. Add the remaining ingredients for the White Sauce and proceed as above.

MUSHROOM SAUCE
Wipe 50g (2 oz) button mushrooms and add to the bowl with the remaining ingredients for the White Sauce and proceed as above. The mushrooms will be chopped during the blending of the ingredients.

MUSTARD SAUCE
Add 1 tsp of mustard powder to the basic ingredients and proceed as for White Sauce.

BREAD SAUCE ❧   *Serves 6–8*

This may be made with white or wholemeal bread.

1 onion, peeled
6 cloves
1 bay leaf
550 ml (1 pint) milk
100g (4 oz) breadcrumbs (*p. 121*)
25g (1 oz) butter
nutmeg
salt and pepper

Spike the onion with the cloves and stand in a milkpan. Pour over the milk and add the bay leaf. Bring to the boil and then remove from the heat. Leave covered for half an hour. Meanwhile make the breadcrumbs. After 30 minutes of infusion add the breadcrumbs and butter and cook uncovered on the lowest heat for 20 minutes. Remove the onion and bay leaf and season with a couple of gratings of nutmeg, salt and black pepper. This sauce may be re-heated later.

APPLE SAUCE ♉ ⚭   *Serves 4–6*

Serve with roast pork or poultry.

450g (1 lb) cooking apples
3 tbsp water
1 tbsp brown sugar
1 clove
25g (1 oz) butter

Peel and core the apples and use the slicing disc to slice the quartered fruit. Put the apple slices into a heavy-based pan with a close-fitting lid. Add the water, sugar and clove and simmer, covered, for about 5 minutes over a low heat until softened. Fit the steel blade, remove the clove from the apple, add the butter and process until smooth and the butter has melted into the sauce. Serve hot or cold.

MINT SAUCE ⚭   *Serves 6–8*

Traditionally served with roast lamb.

bunch of fresh mint
1 tsp sugar
150ml (¼ pint) malt vinegar

Strip the leaves from the stems, wash in cold water and shake dry. Put into the bowl with the sugar and process until the mint is finely chopped. Add the vinegar and process briefly to mix.

GOOSEBERRY SAUCE ⚭   *Serves 4*

Serve with fish, especially mackerel, or with pork instead of Apple Sauce.

225g (8 oz) fresh gooseberries
or **225g (8 oz) can of gooseberries**
60ml (4 tbsp) water
pinch of freshly grated nutmeg
25g (1 oz) caster sugar
25g (1 oz) butter, softened

Top and tail the gooseberries and put into a medium sized saucepan with the water. Bring to the boil, cover and simmer until softened. Cool slightly and process until puréed. (Pour canned gooseberries straight into the bowl and purée.) Add the nutmeg, sugar (omit from the canned version), and butter, and process until blended. Return to the saucepan and re-heat, stirring until the sugar is dissolved and the butter melted.

TOMATO SAUCE ☙   *Serves 4*

Ideal for pouring over freshly cooked ravioli, spaghetti or fried meat or fish.

1 tbsp oil
1 medium sized onion, peeled and quartered
397g (14 oz) can of tomatoes
2 tbsp tomato purée
$\frac{1}{2}$ tsp salt
black pepper
$\frac{1}{2}$ tsp mixed herbs or basil
bay leaf

Roughly chop the onion in the processor bowl and fry in a pan over a gentle heat in the oil until softened but not browned. Put all the remaining ingredients, except the bay leaf, into the processor and process until well blended. Pour over the onion, add the bay leaf and simmer uncovered for 10 minutes while cooking the pasta or meat. Discard bay leaf before pouring over the pasta or serving with meat.

BOLOGNESE SAUCE ☙ ♙   *Serves 4*

Serve with pasta or as a basis for other dishes.

1 onion, peeled and quartered
2 cloves garlic
1 tbsp olive oil
1 green pepper, de-seeded and quartered
2 sticks celery
150g (6 oz) button mushrooms
700g (1$\frac{1}{2}$ lb) minced beef
550ml (1 pint) beef stock
2 tbsp tomato purée
1 tsp mixed herbs
1 tbsp mushroom ketchup
salt and black pepper

Process the onion, garlic and pepper until coarsely chopped. Without removing the vegetables remove the steel blade and fit the slicing disc and slice the celery. Heat the oil in a large, heavy-based saucepan. Fry the vegetables until softened but not browned, stirring frequently. Brown the minced meat with the vegetables. Slice the mushrooms and add to the sauce with the remaining ingredients. Bring to the boil, cover and simmer over a gentle heat for an hour.

CURRY SAUCE &

This sauce may be used as a vegetarian curry sauce over boiled rice, or as a hot sauce poured over hardboiled eggs. Alternatively, use as a cooking sauce with chicken joints or cubes of beef or lamb, and add to the browned meat at the stage marked with an asterisk.* Casserole in a medium oven for an hour.

1 large onion, peeled and quartered
2 cloves garlic
1 tbsp oil
2 carrots
3 sticks of celery
1 green pepper, de-seeded and quartered
1 cooking apple, peeled and cored
1 tbsp curry powder
1 tsp cumin
397g (14 oz) can of tomatoes
2 tbsp mango chutney
2 tbsp tomato purée
150ml (¼ pint) stock
25g (1 oz) sultanas
bay leaf
salt and pepper

Use the steel blade to chop the onion and garlic. Heat the oil in a large lidded frypan and gently fry the onion and garlic until softened but not browned. Cut the remaining vegetables and apple into chunks and process until well chopped. Add to the frypan and cook for a couple of minutes over a low heat. Stir in the curry powder and cumin. Put the contents of the can of tomatoes into the bowl with the chutney and tomato purée. Process until smoothly blended then pour over the vegetables. Add the stock, sultanas, seasoning and bay leaf,* bring to the boil then simmer for half an hour. Discard bay leaf before serving.

NUTTY AVOCADO DIP   *Serves 4 as a starter*

Handful of fresh parsley
25g (1 oz) shelled walnuts
1 tbsp lemon juice
2 ripe avocados
200g (7 oz) cream cheese
salt and pepper

Remove the stalks from the washed parsley and process until finely chopped. Add the walnuts and chop roughly. Add the lemon juice. Halve the avocados, remove the stones and spoon the flesh into the bowl. Add the cream cheese and seasoning and blend until smooth. Spoon or pipe into 4 ramekin dishes and garnish with half a walnut. May be made a couple of hours before serving – any longer and the surface will discolour.

TARAMASALATA   *Serves 4 as a starter*

1 small onion, peeled and quartered
100g (4 oz) smoked fish roe
50g (2 oz) stale bread, soaked in water
300ml ($\frac{1}{2}$ pint) olive oil
juice of 2 lemons (4 tbsp)

Process the onion until very finely chopped. Add the roe and process until smooth. Squeeze the water from the bread and add the bread to the roe with the oil and lemon juice. Process until smooth. Store in the refrigerator until needed. Serve with warm pitta bread.

HUMMUS   *Serves 4–6 as a starter*

75g (3 oz) chick peas
1 lemon
2 cloves garlic
3 tbsp olive oil
salt and pepper
fresh parsley

Soak the peas overnight in 1 litre (2 pints) water. Next morning drain the peas, cover with water, bring to the boil and simmer for 2-3 hours until softened. Do not allow the water to boil away, and top up the level if necessary. Drain the peas, reserving 2 tbsp of the liquor. Use the processor to chop finely the lemon zest (see p. 125). Squeeze the juice of half the lemon. Put the peas, the lemon zest and juice, garlic, oil and seasoning into the bowl and process until smoothly blended. Serve either in one large bowl or in individual bowls garnished with chopped parsley (p. 124). Serve with pitta bread.

CHEESE & ONION DIP ɞ   *Serves 6–8*

½ packet of dried onion soup mix
4 tbsp plain yoghurt
225g (8 oz) cottage cheese
salt and pepper
chopped chives to garnish

Put the yoghurt and soup mix into the bowl and process until well blended. Allow to stand for 30 minutes. Add the cheese and seasoning and process until smoothly blended. Transfer to a serving bowl and chill. Serve garnished with chopped chives.

STILTON DIP ɞ   *Serves 4–6*

100g (4 oz) Stilton cheese, rind removed
140ml (5 fl oz) plain yoghurt
1 tbsp mayonnaise
salt and pepper

Use the steel blade to chop the Stilton cheese. Add the remaining ingredients and process until smooth. Serve chilled garnished with the pale green leaves from a stick of young celery.

PINEAPPLE CHEESE DIP ɞ   *Serves 6–8*

220g (7 oz) can of pineapple pieces, drained
1 small or ½ large green pepper, de-seeded and quartered
225g (8 oz) cottage cheese
salt and pepper

Reserve a couple of pieces of pineapple for garnish. Put the remaining pieces into the bowl and process until roughly chopped. Remove from the bowl. Add the green pepper and chop coarsely. Add the cheese, pineapple pieces and seasoning and process until the pineapple and pepper are finely chopped. Serve chilled in a bowl garnished with the pineapple pieces.

TOMATO & ANCHOVY DIP ✎   *Serves 4*

225g (8 oz) tomatoes, skinned and de-seeded
50g (2 oz) can anchovy fillets, drained
4 tbsp yoghurt
1 tsp sugar
2 tbsp tomato purée
pinch of basil

Process the tomatoes and anchovy fillets until finely chopped. Add the remaining ingredients and process until smoothly blended. Garnish with a slice of lemon.

Supper dishes

To many people supper dishes are light snacks to be thrown together in a trice; to others they are a less expensive way of satisfying the family than meat and two veg. Some of the following recipes will also make tasty starters or party nibbles.

NUTTY CHEESE BITES ✌ *Makes 24*

100g (4 oz) hazelnuts
150g (6 oz) Stilton cheese
3 tbsp cream
black pepper
salt
500g (1 lb) flaky pastry
1 egg, separated

Coarsely chop the nuts in the food processor. Add the Stilton, cream and seasoning and blend to form a fine paste. Roll out the pastry and cut 24 pieces measuring 5cm (2 in) square. Spoon a little of the mixture into one half of the square, moisten the edges with the beaten egg white, fold in half and seal firmly. Repeat until all the mixture is used up. Place the pastry envelopes on a greased baking sheet and brush with the beaten egg yolk. Bake for 15-20 minutes at 200°C, 400°F, Gas Mark 6.

FRIED CHEESE PUFFS ✍   *Makes 18*

1 onion, peeled and quartered
225g (8 oz) cheese, cubed
6 eggs
50g (2 oz) plain flour
1 tsp baking powder
salt and pepper
oil for deep frying

Put the onion into the bowl and process until finely chopped. Add the cheese and process until coarsely chopped. Add all the remaining ingredients except the oil and process until well blended. Heat the oil until very hot then drop spoonfuls of the batter into the oil, fry for a few minutes until golden brown, drain and serve with tomato sauce (p. 44). Fry six at a time.

FRIED CAMEMBERT ✍   *Makes 8 cheesy fries*

1 round of Camembert cheese
1 egg, beaten
100g (4 oz) breadcrumbs (*p. 121*)
oil for deep frying

If not already portioned, cut the cheese into 8 segments. With a sharp knife cut the white rind from the cheese. Dip each piece into the egg, then into the breadcrumbs, pressing the crumbs into the cheese. If there are any gaps in the coating, repeat the crumbing. Deep fry the cheeses in very hot oil until golden brown, drain and serve immediately with crisp French bread or cheese biscuits.

SPANISH OMELETTE ♀ ✍   *Serves 1–2*

Various cooked vegetables are suggested, but this is really a dish to use up leftovers.

A selection of cooked vegetables such as potatoes, carrots, green beans, peas or sweetcorn
1 clove garlic
25g (1 oz) garlic sausage or ham, cubed
½ fresh green or red pepper, de-seeded and quartered
3 eggs

salt and pepper
1 tbsp olive oil

First prepare the vegetables. Potatoes should be halved length-ways. Use the slicing disc to slice the potatoes, carrots, beans and red or green pepper. Transfer to a mixing bowl and stir in the peas or sweetcorn. Fit the steel blade and chop the garlic with the sausage or ham. Add the pepper and chop. Add the eggs with the seasoning and process. Heat the oil in a heavy based frypan. When very hot pour in the egg mixture and reduce the heat to low. Sprinkle the vegetables over. Use a spatula to lift the edges as they set to allow the uncooked mixture to seep underneath. Using oven gloves, invert a large plate over the frypan and flip both together to turn out the omelette, cooked side uppermost. Slide it carefully off the plate back into the frypan and cook the other side briefly. Don't overcook or it will be leathery. Serve with a green salad.

PANCAKES   *Makes 8 small pancakes*

50g (2 oz) butter
100g (4 oz) plain flour
2 eggs
300ml ($\frac{1}{2}$ pint) milk
$\frac{1}{4}$ tsp salt
lard or oil for frying

Melt the butter and allow to cool slightly. Put all the remaining ingredients (except the frying lard or oil) into the bowl, add the butter and process until well blended. If necessary scrape down the sides of the bowl. Pour into a jug. Heat a thin film of oil or fat in an omelette pan or small frypan. When smoking hot pour sufficient batter into the pan to form a thin pancake. Cook on a high heat until golden brown underneath, then either flip the pancake with a spatula or toss. Cook the other side until browned. Turn onto a warm plate if to be used immediately, otherwise interleave with greaseproof paper and cool if to be used later or frozen. To re-heat, place the chosen filling onto the pancake, roll up or fold and re-heat for 20 minutes at 190°C, 375°F, Gas Mark 5.

SAVOURY PANCAKES 🐟 ⚘

Filling for 8 small pancakes

Stuffed pancakes with summertime vegetables

225g (8 oz) boiled ham, cubed
300ml (½ pint) coating white sauce *(p. 41)*
1 tbsp mushroom ketchup
salt and pepper
1 large or 2 small courgettes
25g (1 oz) butter
1 green pepper, de-seeded and quartered
1 red pepper, de-seeded and quartered
pinch of mixed herbs

Put the ham into the bowl and process until coarsely chopped. Stir into the seasoned white sauce, with the mushroom ketchup. Divide between the 8 pancakes and roll up into cigar shapes. Arrange in a greased shallow ovenproof dish. Use the slicing disc to slice the courgettes and fry in the butter in a large sauté pan. Slice the peppers and add to the courgettes. Add the herbs and seasoning then spoon over the pancakes. Cover with aluminium foil and re-heat in a medium oven (190°C, 375°F, Gas Mark 5) for 20 minutes.

Tuna Cream
Mix 300ml (½ pint) coating white sauce (p. 41) with a drained can of tuna, and re-heat as above.

Pancakes Provençale
Add spoonfuls of Ratatouille (p. 78), fold and re-heat as above.

QUICHE LORRAINE 🐟

Serves 4

125g (5 oz) shortcrust pastry *(p. 102)*
75g (3 oz) grated cheese *(p. 122)*
100g (4 oz) streaky bacon
1 egg
150ml (¼ pint) milk
salt and pepper

Grease an 18cm (7 in) flan dish or sandwich tin and line with the pastry. Sprinkle half the cheese over the pastry and put the other half on one side until the end. Roughly chop the bacon and put into the bowl. Add the remaining ingredients and process until the bacon is chopped and the custard well combined. Pour into the flan, sprinkle over remaining cheese and bake for 40 minutes at 200°C, 400°F, Gas Mark 6.

SPINACH FLAN ＆   *Serves 4*

125g (5 oz) wholewheat pastry *(p. 103)*
227g (8 oz) pack of frozen leaf spinach
2 eggs
150ml (¼ pint) single cream
salt and pepper
50g (2 oz) grated cheese *(p. 122)*

Grease an 18cm (7 in) flan dish or sandwich tin and line with the pastry. Thaw the spinach and put into the processing bowl. Add the eggs, cream and seasoning and process until the spinach is well chopped. Pour into the flan, sprinkle with the cheese and bake for 40 minutes at 200°C, 400°F, Gas Mark 6.

PIZZA ＆ ＄   *Serves 4–6*

½ portion of risen basic white bread dough *(p. 107)*
1 tbsp olive oil
1 large or 2 small onions, peeled and quartered
garlic *(optional)*
397g (14 oz) can of tomatoes, drained
2 tbsp tomato purée
1 tsp mushroom ketchup
salt and pepper
½ tsp mixed herbs
175g (6 oz) cheese
50g (1¾ oz) can of anchovy fillets, drained
8-10 stuffed olives

While waiting for the bread to rise make the topping. Put the onion and garlic into the bowl and process until coarsely chopped. Heat the oil in a frypan and fry gently until softened but not browned. Put the tomatoes, purée, mushroom ketchup, seasoning and herbs into the bowl and process until puréed. Add to the onion and simmer until thickened. Cool the mixture. Roll out the dough to form a 23cm (9 in) round and place on a greased baking sheet. Alternatively stand a flan ring on the baking sheet and press the dough to fit. Brush with a little olive oil and spoon the cooled mixture over the pizza, leaving a narrow border all round. Using the slicing disc, thinly slice the cheese and arrange over the tomato topping. Cut the anchovy fillets in half lengthways and arrange in a lattice pattern over the pizza. Halve the stuffed olives and place in between the lattice. Leave in a warm place to prove before baking. Cook at the top of a hot oven, 220°C, 425°F, Gas Mark 7, for 25-30 minutes.

POTATO & MUSHROOM PIE 🍴🍴   *Serves 4*

Fresh parsley
3 cloves garlic
100g (4 oz) butter
salt and black pepper
1kg (2 lb) potatoes
100g (4 oz) button mushrooms
milk

Process the parsley to produce about 2 tbsp of chopped parsley. Add the garlic and process until crushed. Add the butter and ½ tsp salt and process until well blended. Scrape from the bowl and keep to one side. Fit the slicing disc and slice the potatoes very thinly, remove then slice the wiped mushrooms. Rub the base and sides of a wide diameter, fairly shallow dish, with a little of the garlic butter. Layer half the mushrooms into the dish and top with half the potato. Season with black pepper and repeat with the remaining mushrooms and finally arrange a neat lid of potato slices. Sprinkle with black pepper. Melt the garlic butter and pour over the potatoes. Top up with milk, leaving a margin for the liquid to boil up during cooking, otherwise it will boil over. Cover with greased aluminium foil and bake for 1½ hours at 170°C, 325°F, Gas Mark 3. Remove the foil, boost the heat to 200°C, 400°F, Gas Mark 6 and brown for a further half hour.

MOUSSAKA 🍴 🍴 🍴   *Serves 4*

2 aubergines
100g (4 oz) cheese
1 onion, peeled and quartered

1 tbsp olive oil
2 lamb neck fillets (approx.total 1kg/2 lb)
salt and black pepper
mixed herbs
230g (8 oz) can of tomatoes
1 tsp Worcestershire sauce
2 tbsp tomato purée
300ml ($\frac{1}{2}$ pint) coating white sauce *(p. 41)*

Use the slicing disc to slice the aubergines thickly. Put into a large
mixing bowl in layers, salting each layer. Leave to stand for an
hour. Fit the grating disc and grate the cheese. Remove and keep to
one side. Fit the steel blade and coarsely chop the onion. Fry in the
oil in a large frypan until softened but not browned. Cube the lamb
and put into the bowl with the seasoning and a sprinkling of mixed
herbs, and process until finely chopped. Add to the onion and fry
until browned. Add the can of tomatoes, including the juice, Worcestershire sauce and tomato purée. Mix in, bring to the boil and
reduce the heat to a low simmer. Make the white sauce and add 75g
(3 oz) of the cheese, stirring until melted. Rinse the aubergines in a
colander under cold running water. Drain and arrange half in the
bottom of a large, shallow casserole dish. Spoon in the meat
mixture and cover with the remaining aubergines. Pour the cheese
sauce over and sprinkle with the remaining cheese. Cook in a
medium oven (190°C, 375°F, Gas Mark 5) for 30–40 minutes until
cooked through and the top is browned.

CANNELLONI   🍂 🍴   *Serves 4*

Stuffing:
1 small bunch of fennel leaves
1 clove garlic
10g ($\frac{1}{2}$ oz) butter
225g (8 oz) turkey breasts, cut into chunks
75g (3 oz) brown breadcrumbs
1 egg
salt and pepper

12 cannelloni tubes (approx. 100g (4 oz))
175g (6 oz) button mushrooms
300ml ($\frac{1}{2}$ pint) pouring white sauce *(p. 41)*

Put the fennel and garlic into the bowl and chop finely. Fry in the butter until softened but not browned. Process the turkey until coarsely chopped. Add to the frypan and cook until just starting to brown. Remove from the heat. Put the breadcrumbs, egg, seasonings and turkey mixture into the bowl and process until blended. Don't over process. Allow to cool while making the sauce. Slice the mushrooms and stir into the white sauce. Use a teaspoon to fill the cannelloni tubes with the stuffing. Don't leave to stand long as the stuffing will expand and the tubes crack. Lay the tubes in a greased shallow ovenproof dish, preferably rectangular in shape. Spoon over the mushroom sauce and cook for 30 minutes at 190°C, 375°F, Gas Mark 5.

An alternative is to stuff the cannelloni with Bolognese Sauce (p. 44) and pour over a cheese sauce (p. 42).

SAVOURY CHOUX BUNS　　　　*Makes about 16*

1 batch of basic choux pastry *(p. 105), adding*
**　1 tbsp curry powder and ¼ tsp paprika pepper with the flour**

Spoon the pastry in small rounds onto a greased baking tray. Bake at 200°C, 400°F, Gas Mark 6 for 20 minutes, then reduce the heat to 170°C, 325°F, Gas Mark 3, and bake for a further 20 minutes. Allow to cool on a wire rack, making a small hole in each bun, to allow the steam to escape. Cut each bun in half and fill with a choice of fillings.

Fillings: 🍴

Walnut Cheese Put 25g (1 oz) walnuts into the bowl and process until coarsely chopped. Add 150g (6 oz) cream cheese and blend together.

Celery and apple Coarsely chop 4 sticks of celery and a large peeled and cored cooking apple. Add 150g (6 oz) cottage cheese and seasoning and process to blend.

HAM & ASPARAGUS RING 🍴

1 batch of basic choux pastry *(p. 105)*
Filling:
340g (12 oz) can of asparagus cuts and tips

300ml (½ pint) coating white sauce *(p. 41)* **using liquid from can of asparagus**
225g (8 oz) boiled ham, cubed
salt and pepper

Prepare the pastry and, using a tablespoon, form a circle of choux pastry on a greased baking sheet. Bake at 200°C, 400°F, Gas Mark 6, for about 45 minutes until crisp and browned. Slit a couple of holes in the side to allow the steam to escape. Cool on a wire rack and slice in half around the "equator". Spoon in the filling and serve hot or cold. Serve immediately, otherwise the pastry will become soggy.

Filling: Use the drained liquid from the asparagus to form part of the liquid in the white sauce. Put the ham into the bowl and process until coarsely chopped. Add the white sauce, seasoning and asparagus and pulse to mix in.

SAUSAGEMEAT PLAIT ♣   *Serves 4–6*

1 batch of wholewheat pastry *(p. 103)*
1 medium sized onion, peeled and quartered
1 small or half 1 large green pepper, de-seeded and quartered
1 tsp oil
50g (2 oz) salted peanuts
450g (1 lb) pork sausagemeat
salt and pepper
½ tsp dried mixed herbs

Process the onion and green pepper until coarsely chopped. Fry in the oil until softened. Cool slightly. Process the peanuts until coarsely chopped, add the sausagemeat, seasoning, herbs and onion mixture. Process until combined. Roll out the pastry to form a square 40 × 40cm (16 × 16 in). Transfer to a greased, lipped baking sheet. Spoon the sausagemeat mixture down the length of the middle third of the pastry, leaving a 10cm (4 in) border at the top and bottom. Using a sharp knife, cut the left and right hand wings of the pastry into 1.5cm (½ in) strips, angled slightly downwards. Fold the top and bottom borders over the sausagemeat. Starting at the top, fold the strips over the sausagemeat, left over right, until the plaited effect is achieved down the whole length. Bake for 35 minutes at 200°C, 400°F, Gas Mark 6.

Meat, Poultry, Game and Fish

Use your food processor to chop raw or cooked meat, blend a marinade or mix a stuffing; and if you are trying to avoid calorie-laden sauces thickened with flour, use it to purée the vegetables cooked with the meat, to form a deliciously light sauce.

Lovers of Chinese stir-fry can take meat straight from the freezer, cut it into pieces to fit the feed tube, and use the slicing disc to produce slivers of beef, pork or chicken (boned) that cook in seconds in a wok. Remember to remove all fat, sinews and bone before slicing.

That is the same advice when mincing uncooked meat; otherwise the fat and sinews end up wrapped around the drive shaft. When mincing uncooked, thawed meat, cut it into 3cm (1½ in) cubes and process a maximum of 340g (12 oz) at any one time. The longer the motor runs, the finer the texture of the minced (or chopped) meat, so take care not to over-process.

CROWN ROAST OF LAMB ⁊   *Serves 4–6*

Stuffing: **1 lemon**
100g (4 oz) breadcrumbs *(p. 121)*
1 onion, peeled and quartered
1 clove garlic *(optional)*
1 tbsp oil
25g (1 oz) shelled walnuts
1 small or ½ large cooking apple, peeled and cored
salt and pepper

1 crown of lamb, comprising 12 best end of neck chops
12 cutlet frills

Finely chop the lemon zest (p. 125) and in the same bowl make the
breadcrumbs. Transfer to a basin. Put the onion and garlic into the
bowl and process until coarsely chopped. Heat the oil in a small
frypan and fry the onion and garlic over a low heat until softened
but not browned. Put the walnuts into the bowl and process until
coarsely chopped. Roughly cut up the apple into chunks and add to
the bowl. Process until finely chopped. Add the seasoning, bread-
crumb mixture and onion, and process until combined. Stand the
crown in a roasting tin. Season and wrap foil around the tips of the
chops to prevent burning. Spoon the stuffing into the middle and
brush the outside of the crown with cooking oil. Roast for 1¼–1½
hours at 190°C, 375°F, Gas Mark 5. Transfer to a serving dish,
remove the foil and decorate with the cutlet frills.

MARINATED LEG OF LAMB ⁊   *Serves 4–6*

2kg (4 lb) leg of lamb
good bunch of fresh mint
1 tbsp coriander seeds
1 tbsp whole Jamaican peppercorns
150ml (¼ pint) plain yoghurt
1 tbsp cooking oil
2 tbsp whole green cardamom

With a sharp knife stab the lamb with about 20 deep cuts all over its
surface. Wash the mint and strip off the leaves. Process the leaves
until finely chopped. Add the peppercorns and coriander seeds and

process to chop coarsely. Heat the oil in a small frypan with a lid close to hand. Add the cardamom pods and immediately cover while they "pop" in the hot oil. When the popping ceases, remove from the heat and remove the lid. Add the yoghurt to the contents of the bowl, add the slightly cooled oil and cardamom and process to blend. Stand the lamb in a shallow earthenware dish, pour over the marinade and coat the lamb on all sides. Turn once or twice during the marinating time – from 2-6 hours. Transfer to a roasting tin and roast at 190°C, 375°F, Gas Mark 5 for 1½-2 hours, depending on preference.

SPICY CASSEROLE OF LAMB 🐑 🍴   *Serves 4*

50g (2 oz) dried apricots
1 large onion, peeled and quartered
397g (14 oz) can of tomatoes
1 tbsp peanut butter
salt and pepper
1 tbsp oil
700g (1½ lb) lean stewing lamb, cubed
700g (1½ lb) potatoes, peeled

Process the halved apricots until finely chopped. Add the onion and chop coarsely. Add the whole can of tomatoes, peanut butter and seasoning and process to blend. Brown the meat in the oil in a flameproof casserole. Pour the sauce over. Fit the slicing disc, slice the potatoes, and arrange as a lid over the meat. Cook for 1½ hours in a medium oven, 190°C, 375°F, Gas Mark 5.

LAMB PASTIES 🐑 🍴 🐑   *Serves 4–6*

Filling:
1 onion, peeled and quartered
1 tbsp oil
100g (4 oz) carrots, peeled
225g (8 oz) potatoes, peeled
225g (8 oz) lean lamb, cubed
150ml (¼ pint) stock
½ tsp ground mace
salt and pepper

Pastry:
350g (12 oz) shortcrust pastry *(p. 102)*

Process the onion until finely chopped. Gently fry in the oil in a large frypan until softened but not browned. Using the grating disc shred the carrots and potatoes. Add to the frypan and gently fry for a minute. Fit the steel blade and process the meat until finely chopped. Add to the frypan and brown the meat. Add the stock and seasoning and simmer, covered, until cooked. Allow to cool while you prepare the pastry. Divide the pastry into 4 or 6 equal pieces and roll each into thin rounds. Moisten the edges of the pastry and share the meat mixture between the rounds, spooning it into the centre of each. Bring the two edges together and seal. Place on a greased baking sheet, and if wished, brush with beaten egg, and bake for 30-35 minutes at 200°C, 400°F, Gas Mark 6. Serve hot.

LANCASHIRE HOT POT ☺   *Serves 4*

700g (1½ lb) potatoes, peeled
2 large onions, peeled and quartered
700g (1½ lb) stewing lamb, cubed
salt and pepper
300ml (½ pint) lamb stock

Use the slicing disc to slice the potatoes and onions. Layer the meat then the onions, then the potatoes in a casserole, seasoning each layer. Pour over the stock, cover with a lid or foil, and cook for 2 hours at 170°C, 325°F, Gas Mark 3. Remove the foil and bake for a further half an hour, to crisp the potato top.

CIDER BRAISE OF BEEF ☺ ๏   *Serves 6–8*

225g (8 oz) carrots, peeled
175g (6 oz) celery
225g (8 oz) leeks, cleaned
1 tbsp oil
1.5kg (3 lb) rolled brisket of beef
1 clove garlic
550ml (1 pint) cider
salt and pepper
½ tsp dried mixed herbs.

Use the slicing disc to slice the carrots, celery and leeks into the bowl together. Cut the garlic into about 8 thin slivers. With a sharp pointed knife cut 8 slits along the top of the brisket and insert the garlic slivers. Heat the oil in a large frypan or flameproof casserole and brown the meat on all sides. Remove the meat from the pan and add all the vegetables, frying briskly and stirring to prevent sticking. Pour over the cider, season and stand the beef on the vegetables. If using a frypan, transfer the vegetables to an oven-proof casserole with the cider and add the meat. Sprinkle with salt and pepper and the herbs. Cover and cook for about 2 hours at 190°C, 375°F, Gas Mark 5. When cooked remove the beef to a carving dish. Using a slotted spoon, transfer the cooked vegetables to the processing bowl, fitted with the steel blade. Process until smoothly puréed; stir the purée into the cooking liquor, re-heat and adjust seasoning before serving as a sauce with the beef.

BEEF OLIVES ✍ ☕ *Serves 4*

8 thin slices of beef *(ask your butcher to cut the slices for beef olives)*
75g (3 oz) breadcrumbs *(p. 121)*
50g (2 oz) oatflakes
2 onions, peeled and quartered
1 clove garlic *(optional)*
50g (2 oz) butter
225g (8 oz) mushrooms
1 tsp mushroom ketchup
3 sticks celery
295g (10 oz) can of condensed celery soup
water
½ tsp horseradish
1 tsp capers
salt and pepper

Make the breadcrumbs and remove from the bowl. Process one onion and garlic until coarsely chopped. Fry the onion mixture in half the butter until softened but not browned. Process the mush-rooms until coarsely chopped. Add to the bowl the breadcrumbs, oatflakes, chopped onion, mushroom ketchup and seasoning. Pro-cess until well blended. Divide the mixture between the 8 slices of beef, roll up and tie at each end with a piece of string. Brown the beef olives in the remaining butter until browned on all sides, and transfer to an oven-proof casserole. Rinse out the bowl and fit the slicing disc. Slice the other onion and celery and fry in the butter until golden brown. Stir in the can of condensed soup and gradually stir in a can full of water. Add the horseradish, capers and seasoning. Bring to the boil then pour over the beef olives. Cover and cook in the oven for 1½ hours at 190°C, 375°F, Gas Mark 5. Cut and remove the strings before serving.

BEEF SATAY &   *Serves 4*

700g (1½ lb) rump steak
2 tbsp oil
2 tbsp soy sauce
4 tbsp lemon juice
6 tbsp peanut butter
½ tsp chilli powder
salt

Cut the steak into 1cm (½ in) cubes. Process the remaining ingredients until well blended. Coat the meat in the sauce and leave for a minimum of 2 hours, preferably 8 hours. Thread the cubes onto 4 metal skewers and cook over a barbecue or hot grill for 15-20 minutes. Turn frequently and baste with any excess sauce. Serve with fried rice.

BEEFBURGERS &   *Serves 4–8*

1 large onion, peeled and quartered
700g (1½ lb) minced beef
25g (1 oz) oatflakes
1 egg
1 tsp salt
1 tsp chilli sauce
1 tbsp lemon juice
oatflakes, extra

Finely chop the onion. Add all the remaining ingredients and process until well mixed. Sprinkle the extra oatflakes on a clean surface and divide the mixture into 8 equal portions (each weighs around 100g/4 oz). Shape into burgers and coat both sides with oat flakes. Shallow fry, grill or barbecue, turning once. Serve either in a sesame seed bun or with chips.

COTTAGE PIE ✌

This is an ideal way to use up the remains of Sunday's joint. The basic recipe is given below with variations to ring the changes. The quantities given would serve 4.

2 onions, peeled and quartered
50g (2 oz) butter
450g (1 lb) cooked beef, eg brisket
300ml (½ pint) beef stock
salt and pepper
700g (1½ lb) mashed potatoes

Process the onions until coarsely chopped. Fry in the butter until starting to turn brown. Cut the beef into 3cm (1½ in) cubes and process in two batches until coarsely chopped. Add to the onions and brown. Add the stock and seasoning, bring to the boil and transfer to an oven-proof dish. Pipe or fork the potato over the meat. Bake for 20-30 minutes at 230°C, 450°F, Gas Mark 8, until browned on top and heated through.

Variations:
- Add 1 tbsp Worcestershire sauce to the stock.
- Substitute for the stock, 397g (14 oz) can of tomatoes, with a beef stock cube and 3 tbsp tomato purée.
- Add 1 tsp horseradish sauce to the stock.
- Substitute for the stock, 300ml (½ pint) brown ale, plus 1 tsp French mustard and a beef stock cube.

DEVILLED SPARE RIBS ✌   *Serves 4*

1kg (2 lb) pork spare ribs
2 cloves garlic
1 tsp mustard powder
1 tsp curry powder
1 tsp ground ginger
dash of tabasco sauce
2 tbsp Worcestershire sauce

2 tbsp tomato purée
$\frac{1}{2}$ tsp salt
230g (8 oz) can of tomatoes, drained

If the ribs are still attached, separate by cutting between the bones. Put all the remaining ingredients into the bowl and process until the garlic is finely choped and the mixture is well blended. Coat the ribs with the sauce and marinade for 2-8 hours. Cook for 15-20 minutes over a barbecue or under a hot grill. Serve with Egg Fried Rice (p. 82).

LEMON STUFFED PORK CHOPS 🐖 🐟 *Serves 4*

Stuffing:
1 onion, peeled and quartered
1 tbsp oil
$\frac{1}{2}$ lemon
50g (2 oz) breadcrumbs *(p. 121)*
pinch of sage
salt and pepper

4 thick cut pork chops
1 onion, peeled and quartered
1 tbsp oil
225g (8 oz) button mushrooms
salt and pepper
300ml ($\frac{1}{2}$ pint) dry cider

Process the onion until coarsely chopped and soften in the oil over a gentle heat in a small frypan. Cut and finely chop the zest of the $\frac{1}{2}$ lemon (see p. 125). Prepare the breadcrumbs, if necessary, on top of the lemon zest. Add the sage, seasoning and cooked onion. Process to form the stuffing. With a sharp knife cut a pocket in each pork chop, until the point of the knife reaches the bone. With a teaspoon stuff each chop with the mixture. Place in a casserole. Use the slicing disc to slice the second onion, which should be gently fried in the oil until softened. Slice the mushrooms and add to the onions. Season and add the cider. Bring to the boil and pour the sauce over the chops. Cover and cook for about an hour at 180°C, 350°F, Gas Mark 4.

CHICKEN & HAM RAISED PIE ❧ *Serves 4–6*

Filling:
1 lemon
parsley
3 chicken portions
225g (8 oz) uncooked ham, cubed
salt and pepper
2 tbsp water
2 hardboiled eggs
beaten egg

1 batch of hot water crust pastry *(p. 104)*
1 sachet of gelatine
300ml (½ pint) chicken stock

Finely chop the zest of the lemon (see p. 125) and process the parsley in the same bowl until finely chopped. Cut the chicken from the bones, cube and add to the bowl with the ham, juice of lemon and seasoning. Process until coarsely chopped. Remove from the bowl and keep to one side. Make the pastry as directed. Cut a quarter of the pastry and reserve, covered until needed for the lid. Mould the pastry on a greased baking sheet to form a 16cm (6 in) diameter shell, the size of a cake tin. Cut a double thickness of greaseproof paper, the height of the sides of the pie, and tie around the pastry case to hold it in shape. Put half the mixture into the case and arrange the shelled hardboiled eggs in the centre, but not touching. Cover with the remaining meat and sprinkle with the water. Dampen the edges of the case, roll out the remaining pastry to form a lid, place on top of the pie and crimp the edges to form a rim. Cut a small hole in the centre of the lid. Use pastry trimmings to decorate the lid with leaves. Glaze with a little beaten egg, then bake for 20 minutes at 220°C, 425°F, Gas Mark 7, then reduce the heat to 180°C, 350°F, Gas Mark 4 for a further 1½ hours. Remove the pie from the oven and when cool remove the greaseproof paper. Sprinkle the gelatine on the warmed stock and when dissolved pour through the centre hole. Refrigerate to speed up the setting process. When absolutely cold remove from the baking sheet and serve.

CHICKEN WITH WATERCRESS MAYONNAISE
Serves 6

6 chicken breasts, boned and skinned
1 tbsp white wine vinegar
bunch of fresh thyme and parsley sprigs
salt and pepper
slivers of zest of lemon
1 batch of Watercress Mayonnaise *(p. 40)*

Put the chicken breasts into a large, lidded frypan. Half cover with water and add the wine vinegar, herbs, lemon zest and seasoning. Bring to the boil, lower the heat and simmer, covered, for approximately 30 minutes or until thoroughly cooked. Remove the chicken and allow to cool. Strain the cooking liquor and use it for stock. Arrange the chicken on a serving dish and just before serving spoon over the Watercress Mayonnaise and garnish with slices of lemon.

CHILLED CURRIED CHICKEN & *Serves 6*

1 cooked chicken, cold and skinned
1 tbsp oil
1 onion, peeled and quartered
1 tbsp curry powder
150ml (¼ pint) chicken stock
1 tsp tomato purée
1 tbsp lemon juice
2 tbsp apricot jam
300ml (½ pint) good mayonnaise
3 tbsp double cream
green and black grapes for garnish

Strip the chicken from the bones and cut into bite-sized chunks. Process the onion until finely chopped and fry in the oil until softened but not browned. Stir in the curry powder and cook for a few minutes. Stir in the stock, purée, lemon juice and jam, and simmer for 4-5 minutes. Allow to cool. When cold process until smooth. Add the mayonnaise and cream and process until thoroughly blended. Arrange the chicken in the centre of a serving dish and pour the sauce over. Surround with cold cooked rice and garnish with halved de-seeded grapes.

POLLO TONATO ~ &   *Serves 4*

4 chicken breasts, boned
300ml (½ pint) water
1 tbsp lemon juice
1 tsp salt
1 tsp dried tarragon
198g (7 oz) can of tuna in oil, drained
8 tbsp good mayonnaise
2 tbsp lemon juice
salt and pepper
stuffed olives for garnish

Put the water, lemon juice, salt and tarragon into a large lidded frypan and bring to the boil. Add the chicken, cover and reduce to a simmer for 20-30 minutes. Remove the cooked chicken from the pan, reserving the liquor for stock. Put the tuna, mayonnaise and lemon juice into the bowl and process until smoothly blended. Season to taste and spoon over the cold chicken. Garnish with sliced stuffed olives.

SMOTHERED DRUMSTICKS ~ &   *Serves 4*

1 green pepper, de-seeded and quartered
2 cloves garlic, peeled
1 tbsp chive mustard
1 tbsp peanut butter
salt and pepper
8 chicken drumsticks

Process the pepper and garlic until finely chopped. Add the remaining sauce ingredients and process until blended to a paste. Coat the chicken drumsticks with the paste and grill for 20 minutes, turning once. Serve with rice and green salad.

SWEET & SOUR CHICKEN &   *Serves 4*

1 onion, peeled and quartered
1 green pepper, de-seeded and quartered
1 stick of celery, cut into 4
1 tbsp oil
4 chicken joints
227g (8 oz) can of pineapple slices or chunks
1 tbsp cornflour
4 tbsp wine vinegar
1 tbsp soy sauce
50g (2 oz) brown sugar
salt and pepper

Put the onion, pepper and celery into the bowl and process until coarsely chopped. Brown the chicken joints in the oil in a large lidded frypan. Remove the chicken from the pan and keep on one side. Gently fry the vegetables in the remaining oil until softened but not browned. Drain the pineapple juice from the can into a measuring jug and add sufficient water to make 300ml (½ pint). Put this liquid into the bowl with the pineapple and all the remaining ingredients. Add the fried vegetables and process until the sauce is well blended. Return the chicken to the frypan, pour over the sauce, cover and bring to the boil. Reduce the heat to simmering and cook for 15-25 minutes, depending on the thickness of the chicken.

POUSSIN IN BARBECUE SAUCE &   *Serves 4*

4 poussin, oven ready
1 onion, peeled and quartered
2 cloves garlic, peeled
1 green pepper, de-seeded and quartered
10g (½ oz) butter
397g (14 oz) can of tomatoes
1 tbsp Worcestershire sauce
dash of tabasco
2 tbsp tomato purée
½ tsp salt
½ tsp cayenne pepper

Process the onion, garlic and pepper until coarsely chopped. Fry in the butter in a small frypan until softened. Remove from the heat and cool slightly. Add the remaining sauce ingredients to the bowl and process until well blended. Add the onion mixture and process briefly to mix in. Pour into a large bowl and add the poussins. Turn in the sauce until well coated and leave to marinade for 4-6 hours in a casserole. Pour over any remaining sauce. Cook uncovered in a medium oven for an hour at 190°C, 375°F, Gas Mark 5. Serve with rice with the remaining sauce served in a sauce boat.

ROAST CHICKEN WITH ORANGE STUFFING

Serves 4–6

1 orange
1 onion, peeled and quartered
1 tbsp oil
225g (8 oz) pork sausagemeat
50g (2 oz) long grain rice, cooked
salt and pepper
1.5-2.5kg (3-5 lb) roasting chicken, oven-ready
sprigs of fresh thyme
salt and pepper

Remove the orange zest and finely chop (see p. 125). Add the onion to the bowl and process until finely chopped. Heat the oil in a small frypan and cook the sausagemeat without browning. Cool slightly. Drain off the oil and transfer the sausagemeat to the bowl. Add the rice and seasoning and process to mix. Spoon this stuffing into the neck cavity and put any excess into an ovenproof dish. Stand the chicken on a rack in a roasting tin, sprinkle with salt and pepper and insert the thyme into the body cavity. Cover loosely with aluminium foil and cook on the middle shelf at 190°C, 375°F, gas mark 5 for 25 minutes per 500g (1 lb). Remove the foil for the last hour to crisp the skin. At the same time put the extra stuffing into the oven, covered with foil and cook on a lower shelf. Make a stock from the giblets which can be thickened for the gravy. If wished, the juice of the orange may be added to the gravy, or the orange segments may be used to garnish.

BRAISED GROUSE WITH 🥄 🍴
RED CABBAGE   *Serves 2–4*

25g (1 oz) butter
2 casseroling (old) grouse, cleaned
1 large onion peeled and quartered
2 sticks of celery
1 small or ½ large red cabbage
salt and pepper
550ml (1 pint) Valpolicella *(this leaves a good glassful for the cook)*
2 tbsp tomato purée
bouquet garni

Melt the butter in a flame-resistant casserole or a large frypan.
Brown the grouse on all sides and remove from the pan or
casserole. In the bowl coarsely chop the onion, replace the steel
blade with the slicing disc and slice the celery. Transfer the onion
and celery to the butter and fry until starting to brown. Meanwhile,
remove the stalk from the cabbage and cut into chunks to fit the
feed tube. Slice the cabbage using the disc. Add the onion and
celery and stir in well. If in a frypan, transfer the vegetables to a
casserole. Season and stir in the wine and tomato purée. Add the
bouquet garni and arrange the grouse on the vegetables. Cover and
cook for 2½ hours at 180°C, 350°F, Gas Mark 4. Discard the
bouquet garni and serve with bread sauce (p. 42).

STUFFED MACKEREL 🥄   *Serves 4*

2 large or 4 small mackerel, cleaned and heads removed
75g (3 oz) fresh breadcrumbs *(p. 121)*
1 onion, peeled and quartered
1 cooking apple, peeled, cored and quartered
25g (1 oz) butter
salt and pepper
large pinch of dried dill weed

Thoroughly rinse the fish in clean running water and pat dry with
kitchen paper. Season inside each of the fish. Make the breadcrumbs, if necessary, and remove from the bowl. Put the onion and
apple into the bowl and process until coarsely chopped. Fry these
in the butter in a small frypan until softened. Return to the bowl,

add the breadcrumbs, seasoning and dill, and process until well blended. Divide the mixture between the fish and stuff the cavity. Grease a large piece of aluminium foil, place it on a baking sheet and arrange the mackerel on the foil. Wrap the foil loosely around the fish, sealing the edges, and bake at 190°C, 375°F, Gas mark 5, for 30-45 minutes, depending on the size of the fish.

SALMON MOULD ◈   *Serves 4–6*

1 sachet powdered gelatine
150ml (¼ pint) water
1 tbsp lemon juice
small bunch of chives or parsley
1 red pepper, de-seeded and quartered
439g (15½ oz) can of red salmon
225g (8 oz) cream cheese
150ml (¼ pint) mayonnaise
1 tsp salt
pinch of cayenne pepper
slices of lemon and cucumber to garnish

Heat the water in a saucepan until hot but not boiling. Remove from the heat and sprinkle on the contents of the sachet. Stir briskly until dissolved and allow to cool. Put the chives or parsley into the bowl and process until finely chopped. Add the pepper and chop finely. Add all the remaining ingredients and process until well blended. Add the cooled gelatine liquid and process until well blended. Pour into a fish shaped mould or loaf tin and refrigerate for a number of hours until set. To unmould, dip briefly into hot water then turn out onto a serving dish. Garnish with slices of lemon and cucumber.

Vegetables and Salads

I really thought that my food processor was the answer to one of my biggest cooking problems: how to chop onions without tears. In a trice they are chopped coarsely or finely, all safely enclosed in the plastic bowl, but the moment I start to fry them . . . my eyes stream just the same.

Vegetables can be prepared in seconds using the steel blade, shredding disc or slicing disc to achieve different textures. Below I list the ways of processing the most common vegetables and alternatives are included, as it is generally more convenient to process different types of vegetable into the bowl in one batch without having to change attachments.

STEEL BLADE

When using the steel blade for chopping, only put vegetables of similar texture into the bowl together, otherwise the more fragile ones, such as mushrooms, will be puréed before the celery or pepper is finely chopped. To avoid uneven chopping, it is preferable to cut the vegetables into chunks roughly 2.5cm (1 in) square. As always, take care not to over-process raw vegetables, and use a pulsing action which allows you to check progress before everything is mashed to a pulp. When puréeing cooked vegetables, it may be necessary to scrape smaller quantities from the sides halfway through processing to ensure a smooth texture.

SLICING DISC

When using the slicing disc you may need to trim vegetables or halve them lengthwise to fit the feed tube. **REMEMBER NEVER TO PUSH THE FOOD DOWN THE TUBE WITH YOUR FINGERS: ALWAYS USE THE PLASTIC PUSHER.** The thickness of the slices is governed by how hard you press down – the lighter the pressure the thinner the slice.

SHREDDING/GRATING DISC

Most shredding/grating discs provided with food processors shred vegetables quite finely, although some models provide a coarser disc which produces juliennes (thin sticks) of vegetables such as carrot and other root vegetables. Use the shredding disc to mash boiled potatoes as the steel blade simply reduces them to a glutinous goo. Again, trim vegetables to fit the feed tube. If you press too firmly, very hard vegetables may form grooves and slow down the grating. Relieve the pressure a little and allow the chunks of vegetable to tumble slightly in the tube.

Aubergines, raw	*Slice*, halving lengthways to fit the tube
	Chop, cutting into chunks
Beetroot, cooked	*Slice* or *shred* for salads
raw	*Shred* for soups or casseroles
Cabbage, raw	*Slice* for salads, pickling or for cooking. Quarter, remove hard centre, if necessary cut smaller to fit feed tube
Carrots, raw	*Slice* by cutting into lengths to stand upright in the feed tube. Pack in as many as possible to keep them in place.
	Shred by cutting into lengths which will lie crossways in the feed tube. Stack three-quarters up the tube and process.
	Chop, cutting into chunks
Celery, raw	*Slice* as for carrots
	Chop, cutting into 2.5cm (1 in) lengths

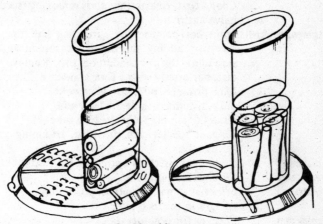

Left: *Shredding carrots*
Right: *Slicing carrots*

Courgettes, raw *Slice*, if necessary cutting larger courgettes lengthways to fit the tube
Shred for salads or stir frying

Cucumber *Slice* – choose a small cucumber or halve a large one lengthways. Peel if wished.

Fennel, raw *Slice*, trimming to fit the tube
Chop, cutting into chunks

Garlic *Chop*, preferably at the same time as another vegetable

Leeks, raw *Slice*, cutting to length as for carrots
Chop, cutting into chunks

Mushrooms, raw *Slice*, packing them in the feed tube with caps facing the sides
Chop, separating the stalks and pulsing for 1 second at a time

Onions, raw *Slice*, halving to fit the tube
Grate, halving to fit the tube
Chop, quartering medium to large onions

Parsnips *Slice*, as for carrots

Peppers *Slice*, first halving lengthways and removing seeds

	Chop, first quartering and removing seeds, halve again
Potatoes, cooked	*Mash* hot potatoes by shredding half the quantity, adding the butter, seasoning and shredding the remainder on top. Remove disc, stir briefly with a fork and serve
	Slice firm new potatoes when cold
raw	*Slice*, trimming to fit the feed tube
	Grate, trimming to fit the feed tube
	Chip, if special disc provided, trimming to fit the tube
Radishes	*Slice*, packing them upright in the feed tube
Swede, raw	*Slice*, as for potatoes
Tomatoes, raw	*Slice* firm small tomatoes, positioning upright in the feed tube
Turnip, raw	*Slice,* as for potatoes

STUFFED TOMATOES   *Serves 4*

1 onion, peeled and quartered
25g (1 oz) butter
100g (4 oz) breadcrumbs *(p. 121)*
75g (3 oz) Danish salami, cut into chunks
pinch of rosemary
4 large firm tomatoes
salt and pepper

Process the onion until finely chopped. Fry the onion in the butter until softened. Prepare the breadcrumbs, if necessary, and add the salami, onion and rosemary. Process until the salami is finely chopped. Cut a lid from each tomato and scoop out the seeds. Season the insides and spoon in the stuffing. Stand on a greased baking sheet and bake for 20 minutes at 190°C, 375°F, Gas Mark 5.

STUFFED MUSHROOMS   *Serves 4*

1 onion, peeled and quartered
2 cloves garlic
25g (1 oz) butter
100g (4 oz) breadcrumbs *(p. 121)*
salt and pepper

½ tsp mixed dried herbs
225g (8 oz) flat cap mushrooms *(a minimum of 2 large mushrooms per person)*

Put the onion and garlic into the bowl and process until finely chopped. In a small frypan fry the onion and garlic in the butter until softened. Make the breadcrumbs, if necessary, and mix in the herbs, seasoning and cooked onion. Remove the stalks from the mushrooms and add the stalks to the mixture, giving them a quick whizz to incorporate them. Place the mushrooms, dish side uppermost, on a greased baking sheet or in the cups of a bun tin. Share the mixture between the mushrooms and cook for 20 minutes in an oven at 190°C, 375°F, Gas Mark 5.

STUFFED AUBERGINES   *Serves 2–4*

1 onion, peeled and quartered
1 clove garlic
2 large aubergines
1 tbsp oil
100g (4 oz) mushrooms, halved
50g (2 oz) brown breadcrumbs *(p. 121)*
salt and pepper
¼ tsp mixed herbs
1 tsp Worcestershire sauce
50g (2 oz) grated cheese

Process the onion and garlic until finely chopped. Using a sharp knife, halve the aubergines and carefully cut away most of the flesh, leaving four shells to be stuffed. Add the flesh to the onion and process until coarsely chopped. Heat the oil in a small frypan and cook the mixture until softened. Put the mushrooms into the bowl and process until coarsely chopped. Add to the frypan and fry gently. Make the breadcrumbs, if necessary, and add to them in the bowl the vegetables from the pan, the seasoning, herbs and sauce. Process to form a smooth stuffing and spoon into the aubergines. Sprinkle with cheese, stand on a baking sheet and bake for 35-40 minutes at 190°C, 375°F, Gas Mark 5.

COURGETTE & TOMATO BAKE ✤ ✤ *Serves 4–6*

700g (1½ lb) courgettes
450g (1 lb) tomatoes, skinned and de-seeded
1 clove garlic
1 tbsp tomato purée
½ tsp ground mace
salt and pepper

Using the slicing disc, finely slice the courgettes. Arrange one third of the courgettes in the base of a shallow casserole. Transfer the remaining courgettes from the bowl to another container for the time being. Fit the steel blade and process the tomatoes and garlic until puréed. Add the seasonings and tomato purée and whizz to blend. Season the courgettes in the casserole and spoon over one third of the tomato sauce. Repeat twice with the remaining courgettes and sauce, cover with aluminium foil and bake for an hour at 190°C, 380°F, Gas Mark 5.

RATATOUILLE ✤ ✤ ✤   *Serves 6 as a starter*

1 aubergine
1 large onion, peeled and quartered
1 clove garlic
small bunch of parsley
3 tbsp olive oil
1 green pepper, quartered and de-seeded
1 red pepper, quartered and de-seeded
450g (1 lb) courgettes
450g (1 lb) small firm tomatoes
salt and black pepper
1 tsp dried mixed herbs

Halve the aubergine lengthways and slice using the slicing disc. Place the slices in a colander, salting each layer in turn. Leave to stand for half an hour. Fit the steel blade and process the onion and garlic until coarsely chopped. Heat the oil in a large flame-proof casserole and gently fry the onion until softened but not browned. Process the parsley until finely chopped (p. 124). Fit the slicing disc and slice the peppers, followed by the courgettes. Transfer the contents of the bowl to the casserole, and stir. Using the slicing disc, slice the tomatoes and add these to the casserole. Rinse the aubergines and add to the rest of the vegetables with the herbs and seasoning, cover and simmer over a low heat for half an hour. If freezing, omit the herbs and garlic.

GERMAN RED CABBAGE ❦

Serves 4–6

1 onion, peeled
50g (2 oz) butter
1 small or ½ large red cabbage
2 cooking apples, peeled and cored
25g (1 oz) sultanas
2 tbsp wine vinegar
2 tbsp brown sugar
salt and pepper
150ml (½ pint) water

Using the slicing disc, slice the onion and fry gently in the butter in a large flame-proof casserole, until softened. Meanwhile quarter the cabbage and remove the thick stem. If necessary, cut into thinner segments to fit the feed tube. Shred using the slicing disc. Slice the apples on top of the cabbage. Add the cabbage and apple to the casserole and stir in. Add all remaining ingredients, bring to the boil, cover and either simmer on the hob over the lowest heat for an hour, or transfer to an oven (180°C, 350°F, Gas Mark 4) for about 1½ hours. This recipe freezes well and is delicious with poultry and game.

ROESTI ❦

Serves 4

1 kg (2 lb) potatoes, unpeeled
75g (3 oz) butter
salt
2 tbsp milk

Cook the potatoes unpeeled *the day before*. Slightly undercook them. The next day peel and use the grating disc to grate the cooked potato. Melt the butter in a lidded Teflon-coated frypan. Add the potato, season and press down with a spatula to form a thick pancake. Sprinkle with the milk and cover with a lid or a large old plate. Ideally there should be very little air space between the top of the Roesti and the lid. As soon as you hear the sound of frying, reduce the heat to minimum and cook for about 30 minutes until a brown crust has formed. Have faith and don't stir the pancake during cooking. Turn out onto a warm serving dish, crust uppermost.

Variation: Fry a finely chopped onion and/or a little chopped bacon in the butter and mix into the potato.

GRATIN DAUPHINOIS   *Serves 6*

100g (4 oz) butter
2 cloves garlic
1kg (2 lb) potatoes, peeled
550ml (1 pint) milk
550ml (1 pint) cream
salt and black pepper

Put the butter and garlic into the bowl and process until the garlic is mashed into the softened butter. Remove from the bowl and fit the slicing disc. Slice the potatoes and rinse, but do not soak them. Butter a large shallow gratin dish using the garlic butter. Layer the well drained potatoes in this dish, seasoning each layer in turn. Add sufficient milk just to cover and half the cream (leaving space for the liquid to rise up during cooking). Cover with aluminium foil and cook for 1½-2 hours at 200°C, 400°F, Gas Mark 6. During this time gradually add the remainder of the cream, stirring to prevent the formation of a hard crust. Remove the foil for the last half hour to allow the top to brown.

POTATOES BOULANGÈRE   *Serves 6*

2 onions, peeled and halved
1 tbsp oil
1.25kg (2½ lb) potatoes, peeled
300ml (½ pint) chicken stock
salt and pepper
25g (1 oz) butter, melted

Using the slicing disc slice the onions thickly. In a large saucepan fry the onion in the oil until softened. If necessary cut the potatoes to fit the feed tube. Slice thickly and add to the onion. Pour in the stock and season. Bring to the boil then spoon into a large shallow casserole, arranging a neat layer of potato slices on the top. Brush with the melted butter and cook at the top of a medium oven (180°C, 350°F, Gas Mark 4) for an hour. Garnish with chopped parsley.

DUCHESS POTATOES 🌸 🍃   *Serves 6*

1kg (2 lb) peeled potatoes
25g (1 oz) butter
salt and pepper
freshly grated nutmeg
1 egg, beaten

Cut the potatoes into chunks which will ultimately fit the feed tube. Boil in salted water until softened. Drain. Put the butter into the processor bowl and fit the grating disc. Feed the hot potatoes through the tube and grate into the bowl. Remove the grating disc and ease the steel blade through the potato mixture into position. If you can't manage this, remove the potato mixture while you fit the blade. Add the seasonings and egg then process briefly until well blended. Pipe or spoon pyramids of the mixture onto a greased baking sheet. Brush lightly with melted margarine and brown in the top of a hot oven or under the grill. The pyramids may be prepared in advance and re-heated at the last minute. If freezing, open freeze then store in a polythene bag.

ALMOND POTATO CAKES 🍃   *Serves 4–6*

450g (1 lb) duchess potato mixture *(above)*
seasoned plain flour
1 egg, beaten
50g (2 oz) almonds

Finely chop the almonds. Divide the mixture into 12 equal portions. Pat into flat rounds. Dip each into the flour, then the egg and finally the almonds. Deep fry until golden brown, drain and serve.

POTATO NESTS 🍴 *Serves 4*

2 very large potatoes, peeled
lemon juice
75g (3 oz) unsalted butter
150ml (¼ pint) oil
salt and pepper

Cut the potatoes into chunks to fit the feed tube. Heat the butter and oil in a large deep frypan. Use the shredding disc to shred the potatoes. Remove the potato shreds and pat sufficient into a burger shape. Sprinkle it with lemon juice and, using a fish slice, slide into the pan. Repeat with the remaining potato. Fry until crisp and brown, remove using the slice. Drain and season just before serving piping hot.

EGG FRIED RICE 🍴 🍴 🍴 *Serves 4*

225g (8 oz) cooked long grain rice
1 onion, peeled and quartered
1 red pepper, de-seeded and quartered
1 tbsp oil
2 sticks celery
1 tbsp soy sauce
1 egg
salt and pepper
chopped parsley to garnish

Ensure that the cooked rice is well drained. Put the onion and red pepper into the bowl and process until coarsely chopped. Remove the steel blade and fit the slicing disc. Slice the celery. Heat the oil in a large deep frypan and, when very hot, stir in the chopped vegetables. Stir fry over a high heat until the vegetables are cooked, but still retain their bite. Meanwhile re-fit the steel blade and process the egg, seasoning and soy sauce until well blended. Add the rice to the frypan and continue to fry over a high heat, stirring briskly. When heated through, stir in the egg mixture and continue stirring until the egg is cooked. Serve garnished with chopped parsley.

LEMON GLAZED CARROTS 🥄 🍽️ *Serves 6–8*

2 lemons
1kg (2 lb) carrots
2 tbsp brown sugar
chicken stock
4 tbsp butter
salt and black pepper
freshly chopped parsley

Finely chop the zest of lemon (see p. 125). Fit the slicing disc and slice the carrots. Put the chopped lemon zest, carrots, sugar, butter and seasoning into a heavy based pan. Add sufficient chicken stock barely to cover. Simmer gently uncovered for about 35 minutes until the carrots are tender and the liquid almost completely evaporated, leaving behind a lemony sauce. Take care that the pan does not boil dry. Serve hot garnished with chopped parsley.

COLESLAW 🥄 🍽️ 🍽️ *Serves 6–8*

Dressing:
1 clove garlic
half a lemon
1 tbsp wine vinegar
5 tbsp mayonnaise
142ml (5 fl oz) carton plain yoghurt
2 tsp grainy French mustard

Slaw:
1 small or ½ a large white cabbage
3 sticks celery
2 carrots
bunch of spring onions, trimmed

Put the garlic into the bowl and process to chop finely. Remove and discard the pips from the lemon, cut into half and process with the garlic until finely chopped. Add all the remaining dressing ingredients and process until well blended. Pour into a large serving bowl. Don't bother to wash out the processor bowl. Quarter the cabbage and remove the thick stem. Cut into segments to fit the feed tube. Fit the slicing disc and use to shred the cabbage.

Transfer the cabbage to the serving bowl if the processing bowl becomes too full. Slice the celery and spring onions. Fit the shredding disc and grate the carrots. Put all the vegetables into the serving bowl and mix in with a fork, tossing them in the dressing until well coated.

CARROT & RAISIN SALAD ⚘   *Serves 4*

225g (8 oz) carrots, peeled
25g (1 oz) raisins
2 tbsp vinaigrette *(p. 39)*

Grate the carrots using the shredding disc. Turn into a serving bowl and mix in the raisins and vinaigrette. If left overnight, the raisins will plump up as they absorb the vinaigrette.

CUCUMBER SALAD ⚘ ⚘   *Serves 4*

142ml (5 fl oz) carton plain yoghurt
salt and pepper
2 tbsp lemon juice
pinch of dill
1 cucumber

Put the yoghurt, seasoning, lemon juice and dill into the bowl and process until well blended. Remove the steel blade and fit the slicing disc. Trim the cucumber into lengths to fit the feed tube, slicing lengthways if too thick. Slice the cucumber thinly into the dressing then turn out into a serving dish. Toss the cucumber to ensure thorough coating.

APPLE & CELERY SALAD ⚘ ⚘   *Serves 4*

vinaigrette *(p. 39)*
1 small head of celery
1 green pepper, quartered and de-seeded
2 red-skinned dessert apples
75g (3 oz) walnut halves
100g (4 oz) Edam cheese

Using the slicing disc slice the celery and green pepper. Quarter and core the unpeeled apples and slice. Toss in the vinaigrette with the walnut halves. Fit the grating disc, grate the cheese and sprinkle over the salad. Toss well to ensure that the apple doesn't discolour.

FENNEL & RED PEPPER ✿   *Serves 4*

1 red pepper, halved and de-seeded
2 cloves garlic
4 tbsp olive oil
2 tbsp wine vinegar
450g (1 lb) small bulbs of fennel
1 tsp brown sugar
light sprinkling of paprika
salt and black pepper

Use the slicing disc to slice the pepper and garlic. Cook both in the oil and vinegar in a frypan over a gentle heat, for about 15 minutes until softened. Trim the fennel and slice. Boil in a pan of salted water for 5 minutes. Drain and arrange in a shallow serving dish. Stir the sugar, paprika and salt into the red pepper, then arrange over the fennel. Spoon over the juices and add a couple of turns of freshly ground black pepper. Serve cold.

MUSHROOM & MINT SALAD ✿ ✿   *Serves 4*

1 tsp coriander seeds
bunch of fresh mint
1 small onion, peeled
4 tbsp red wine vinegar
5 tbsp olive oil
salt and black pepper
225g (8 oz) button mushrooms

Put the coriander, mint leaves and onion into the bowl and process until finely chopped. Add the wine vinegar, oil and seasoning and process briefly to blend. Remove the steel blade and fit the slicing disc. Pack the mushrooms into the tube, caps facing outwards, and slice. Arrange in a serving dish and cover with the dressing.

Desserts

In moments fruit can be whizzed into a purée to flavour ice-cream, sorbets, mousses and fools. What quicker pudding than a drained tin of peaches puréed with a carton of cream? The following recipes are a little more adventurous, but a few tips may help.

Purée
When using fruit with seeds such as raspberries, gooseberries or blackcurrants, it is worth taking the trouble to sieve the puréed fruit to remove the seeds.

Ice-creams
If your food processor doesn't have a special ice-cream making attachment, you can still use it to break down the ice crystals in the semi-frozen mixture. After processing to remove the grainy texture, the mixture will freeze down a second time to make a velvety smooth ice-cream.

Pastries
Use the different pastries described in Chapter 12 to make homely pies and flans or more elegant desserts such as Profiteroles (p. 96).

GOOSEBERRY SORBET

Serves 4–6

550ml (1 pint) unsweetened gooseberry purée, sieved
350g (12 oz) caster sugar
juice of 1 lemon

Put all the ingredients into the bowl and process until well mixed. Pour into a plastic container and freeze for 2 hours. Return to the bowl and process until smooth. Return to the container or mould and freeze solid. Store covered until ready for use. To serve, unmould or use a scoop. Decorate with chopped nuts, if wished.

FRUIT COULIS

This tangy fruit sauce is an ideal way to use up a glut of fruit or the results of an over-enthusiastic pick-your-own session. Not only does it take up less space in the freezer, but also if frozen in small quantities it makes a splendid topping for vanilla ice-cream, or a fruity addition to plain yoghurt. Try some of these ideas: raspberry coulis poured over peaches and ice-cream; blackcurrant coulis poured over strawberry mousse; apricot coulis drizzled over a cream filled meringue, topped with chopped hazelnuts; gooseberry coulis poured over banana and ice-cream.

350g (12 oz) soft fruit such as strawberries, raspberries, peaches, apricots, plums *(gooseberries should first be poached in a little water)*
sufficient icing sugar to sweeten
1 tbsp liqueur *(optional)*

Purée the fruit and pass through a sieve to remove the seeds and/or skins. Return to the clean bowl. Add icing sugar, a spoonful at a time to taste, and if the coulis is to be used immediately, add a tablespoon of brandy or suitable liqueur, e.g. Cointreau with strawberries, Crème de Cassis with blackcurrants. Omit the liqueur if the coulis is to be frozen, adding it just before serving.

PEACH ICE-CREAM ✍   *Serves 4–6*

3 egg yolks
50g (2 oz) caster sugar
284ml (10 fl oz) double cream
1kg (2 lb) fresh peaches

Put the egg yolks, sugar and cream into the bowl and process until well blended. Pour into a thick based saucepan and stir continuously over a medium heat until thickened. Do not boil. Remove from the heat. Plunge the peaches into a bowl of boiling water and after 30 seconds scoop out of the water and plunge into cold water. The skins should now be easy to remove. Cut in half, remove the stone and cut the flesh into quarters. Process half the peaches until puréed and add to the cream mixture. Repeat with the remaining peaches. Stir well then pour into a plastic container. When absolutely cold transfer the container to the freezer and freeze the ice-cream. When firm, return the ice-cream to the bowl, in batches, and process to break down the ice crystals. Return to a clean container and freeze solid.

PEACH CASSATA ✍   *Serves 8*

You will need a freezer for this recipe.

1 batch of peach ice-cream *(above)*
1 batch of gooseberry sorbet *(p. 87)*
150ml (¼ pint) double cream
2 tsp chopped angelica
50g (2 oz) dried apricots
25g (1 oz) flaked almonds

Chill a large loaf tin. Line the base and sides with firm peach ice-cream. Re-freeze until solid. Pack a layer of gooseberry sorbet into the hollow, leaving a hollow in the centre of this second layer to take the cream filling. Re-freeze until solid. Put the dried apricots into the bowl and process until finely chopped. Add the angelica and almonds and chop. Remove from the bowl and add the cream. Process until thickened. Return the chopped ingredients and pulse to blend. Spoon this mixture into the centre of the cassata. If there is any peach ice-cream or gooseberry sorbet left over, use to form a "lid" to the cassata. Return to the freezer and freeze until solid. To unmould, dip the tin briefly in warm water, then invert on a serving dish. Decorate with whipped cream and angelica. Serve in slices.

APRICOT ICE-CREAM   *Serves 6*

1 orange
450g (16 oz) can of apricots
300ml (½ pint) double cream
2 tbsp milk
50g (2 oz) icing sugar

Sauce:
150ml (¼ pint) syrup from apricots
1 tsp arrowroot
4 tbsp apricot jam
blanched almonds for decoration

Finely chop the zest of the orange (see p. 125). Drain the apricots, reserving the syrup. Process the apricots until puréed, add the cream, milk and icing sugar, and process again to blend. Pour into a plastic container and freeze. When firm, return to the processor in batches and process until smooth. Re-freeze until firm. Put the apricot syrup (150ml/¼ pint) into the bowl with the juice of the orange, the arrowroot and the apricot jam. Process until well blended, pour into a small pan and heat until thickened, stirring occasionally. Allow to cool and pour over the ice-cream and decorate with the almonds.

PINEAPPLE CHOC DELIGHT   *Serves 4–6*

This is a delicious, but rather rich dessert.

100g (4 oz) plain chocolate
275g (8 oz) can of pineapple chunks, drained
125ml (¼ pint) double cream
125ml (¼ pint) single cream
2 tbsp brandy or kirsch

Reserve 2 squares of chocolate and put them in the fridge. Melt the remaining chocolate in a bowl over a pan of hot water. Remove from the heat and allow to cool slightly. Process the pineapple until puréed. Remove from the bowl and rinse the bowl. Put the two creams into the bowl and process until thickened but not over-whipped. Add the melted chocolate and pineapple and brandy or kirsch and blend with short pulses. Spoon into serving dishes and chill. Wash out the bowl and rinse in cold water. Dry carefully and fit the steel blade. Take the remaining chocolate from the fridge, break into 4 chunks and process until finely chopped. Sprinkle this "grated" chocolate over the dessert before serving.

STRAWBERRY CREAM MOUSSE   *Serves 4–6*

1 sachet gelatine
6 tbsp water
450g (1 lb) strawberries
225g (8 oz) curd cheese
2 eggs, separated
50g (2 oz) caster sugar
150ml (¼ pint) double cream

Put the water into a cup and sprinkle on the gelatine. Stand the cup in a pan of hot water until the gelatine is dissolved. Wipe and hull the strawberries, reserving a few for decoration. Put into the bowl and purée. Add the cheese and process until well blended. Add the egg yolks, sugar, cream and dissolved gelatine and blend well together. Whisk the egg whites until they form stiff peaks, and with one short burst incorporate them into the strawberry mixture. Pour into a mould and leave to set in the refrigerator. To unmould, dip for a few seconds in hot water and turn out onto a serving dish. Decorate with whipped cream and fresh strawberries.

STRAWBERRY SHORTBREAD   *Serves 4–6*

2 whole shortbread circles *(p. 119)*
350g (12 oz) fresh strawberries, wiped and hulled
300ml (½ pint) double cream

Stand one of the shortbread circles on a serving plate. Process the cream until thickened. Spread half over the shortbread circle on the plate. Scrape the remainder from the bowl and reserve for the time being. Fit the slicing disc. Reserve six strawberries for decoration and slice the remainder. Arrange the slices over the cream and top with the second circle of shortbread, if possible aligning the scored segments of the two circles. Spoon or pipe the remaining cream over the top and decorate with a strawberry on each segment. Refrigerate for 2-6 hours before serving.

BLACKCURRANT CHEESECAKE   *Serves 6–8*

This may also be made with gooseberries or raspberries

450g (1 lb) blackcurrants (or 300ml/½ pint purée)
1 tbsp water
100g (4 oz) caster sugar
100g (4 oz) digestive biscuits
100g (4 oz) muesli
75g (3 oz) butter, melted
126g (4 oz) carton cottage cheese
227g (8 oz) packet of full fat cream cheese
150ml (½ pint) double cream
2 eggs
1 tbsp lemon juice
sachet gelatine

Simmer the fruit and water in a heavy based pan. When cooked transfer to the bowl and purée. Sieve the purée to remove the seeds and skins. Stir into the purée 75g (3 oz) of the sugar. Allow to cool. Wash the bowl and reduce the biscuits to crumbs (p. 121). Add the muesli and pulse to mix. Add the melted butter and process to form a biscuit paste. Line a 20cm (8 in) cake tin with aluminium foil over the base and up the sides. Press the biscuit paste into the cake tin with the back of a metal spoon. Refrigerate to set. Put the two cheeses into the bowl and process until smooth. Pour in the cream through the feed tube, with the motor running, until combined. Scrape down the sides if necessary. Separate the eggs but keep the two whites separate from each other as only one is required for this recipe. Add the two egg yolks and the remaining sugar to the bowl and process until well mixed. Put the lemon juice and 1 tbsp water into a small bowl. Sprinkle over the gelatine and leave to stand for 10 minutes. Then stand the bowl in a pan of simmering water and leave for a few minutes until the gelatine is dissolved. Pour *half* the fruit purée into the cheese mixture and add the gelatine liquid. Process until well mixed. There must be no marbling effect so scrape down the sides to ensure thorough blending. Whisk one of the egg whites until stiff and scrape into the bowl. Pulse once or twice to mix in the egg white. Pour the mixture into the prepared cake tin and leave in the refrigerator to set. To serve, lift the cheesecake from the tin, using the foil as support, and stand it on a serving plate. Use a sharp knife to cut the foil away, leaving only a disc underneath. Serve the remaining fruit purée in a jug or poured over the cheesecake.

LEMON CRUNCH   *Serves 4–6*

225g (8 oz) ginger biscuits
50g (2 oz) butter, melted
1 lemon
150ml (¼ pint) double cream
25g (1 oz) caster sugar
175g (6 oz) can of evaporated milk

Process the biscuits to make crumbs (p. 121). Add the melted butter and process to form a biscuit paste. Grease a china flan dish (16cm/6 in) and press a crust of biscuit paste over the base and sides of the dish. Refrigerate until set. Finely chop the zest of the lemon (see p. 125), first cleaning the bowl. Squeeze the juice of the lemon and reserve. Add the cream, sugar and evaporated milk to the bowl. Process for 30 seconds to mix in the chopped zest of lemon. Strain the lemon juice into the bowl and process until the mixture thickens. Spoon into the prepared flan dish and refrigerate to set. Serve chilled, sprinkled with brown sugar to decorate if wished.

BAKED STUFFED PEACHES   *Serves 4*

50g (2 oz) Brazil nuts
8 Abbey Crunch biscuits, halved
25g (1 oz) caster sugar
25g (1 oz) mixed candied peel
50g (2 oz) butter, softened
4 large firm peaches
sherry *(optional)*

Using the steel blade roughly chop the nuts. Add the biscuits and reduce to crumbs (p. 121). Add the sugar and peel and mix with a short pulse. Add the butter and mix to a stiff paste. Cut the peaches in half, twist to remove the stone from one half and use a sharp knife to ease out the stone from the other. Spoon the mixture into the eight halves and stand each in the cups of a bun tin. Spoon a little sherry over each peach and bake for 15 minutes at 180°C, 350°F, Gas Mark 4. Delicious hot or cold.

APPLE AND BANANA PIE   *Serves 4–6*

175g (6 oz) sweet shortcrust pastry *(p. 103)*
2 under-ripe bananas
450g (1 lb) cooking apples
75g (3 oz) caster sugar
good pinch of mixed spice

Prepare the shortcrust pastry. Fit the slicing disc, peel and slice the bananas. Peel and core the apples, quarter and slice. Mix the sugar with the spice. Arrange the apple and banana in alternate layers in a greased pie dish, sprinkling each layer with the spiced sugar. Cover with the pastry, cut steam vents and decorate with leaves cut from the pastry off-cuts. Brush with milk or beaten egg and milk and bake for 30 minutes at 200°C, 400°F, Gas Mark 6.

SWISS PLUM FLAN 🐎   *Serves 6–8*

350g (12 oz) shortcrust pastry *(p. 102)*
450g (1 lb) ripe plums
25g (1 oz) hazelnuts
2 eggs
150ml (¼ pint) milk (or half milk and half cream)
3 tbsp caster sugar
1 tbsp cornflour

Line with the pastry a greased 22cm (9 in) flan ring, or flan tin with
a removable base. Prick the base of the pastry with a fork. Finely
chop the nuts using the steel blade. Sprinkle the nuts over the
pastry. Halve the plums and remove the stones. Arrange them cut
sides uppermost over the nuts. Make the custard by placing all the
remaining ingredients into the bowl and processing until well
blended. Pour over the plums, if necessary spooning the custard
into the "cups" of the plums. Bake in a pre-heated oven (220°C,
425°F, Gas Mark 7) for 25-30 minutes. If using a china flan dish
you may need additional cooking time to ensure the base is well
cooked – it helps to stand it on a pre-heated baking sheet during
cooking. Serve cold with whipped cream.

APPLE & MINCEMEAT LATTICE 🐎 *Serves 4–6*

225g (8 oz) sweet shortcrust pastry *(p. 103)*
450g (l lb) cooking apples
25g (1 oz) butter
1 egg yolk
1 tbsp caster sugar
2 tbsp brandy
4 heaped tbsp best mincemeat

Line a greased 20cm (8 in) loose-bottomed flan tin with three-
quarters of the pastry. Prick the pastry base and line with foil or
greaseproof paper filled with baking beans. Bake blind for about
15 minutes, or until almost cooked, at 200°C, 400°F, Gas Mark 6.
Remove the foil or greaseproof paper and bake for a further 5-10
minutes until the base is firm and dry. Remove from the oven but

leave the case in the tin. Increase the heat to 230°C, 450°F, Gas Mark 8. Peel, core and quarter the apples. Fit the slicing disc and slice the apples. Melt the butter in a heavy based, lidded pan and add the apples. Cook covered over a medium heat until the apples are softened – about 15 minutes. Shake the pan occasionally to prevent burning. No steam should escape during cooking. Fit the steel blade and add the apples, egg yolk, sugar and 1 tbsp of the brandy. Purée until well blended, scraping the bowl if necessary. Spread the apple purée over the base of the flan. Stir the remaining brandy into the mincemeat and spoon over the apple. Roll out the remaining pastry, cut into strips and arrange in a lattice pattern over the mincemeat. Bake for 20-25 minutes or until the pastry lattice is golden brown. Serve hot or cold.

HEREFORD TREACLE TART 🍂 🌱   *Serves 4–6*

200g (8 oz) shortcrust pastry *(p. 102)*
1 lemon
1 cooking apple
8 tbsp golden syrup
50g (2 oz) white breadcrumbs *(p. 121)*
25g (1 oz) brown sugar
½ tsp ginger

Line a greased 18cm (7 in) pie plate with three-quarters of the pastry, reserving the trimmings. Chop the zest of the lemon (see p. 125) in the bowl. Remove the steel blade and fit the shredding disc. Quarter and core the apple and grate into the bowl. In a small pan melt the golden syrup over a low heat. Add the remaining ingredients, including the lemon rind, grated apple and the strained juice of the lemon. Stir well to mix then spread over the pastry, leaving a border around the edge. Roll out the remaining pastry and cut into strips. Arrange over the tart in a lattice and bake at 190°C, 375°F, Gas Mark 5 for 25 minutes.

RASPBERRY RING ✤   *Serves 6–8*

1 batch of choux pastry *(p. 105)*
300ml (½ pint) double cream
450g (1 lb) fresh raspberries

Bake a choux ring as described in Ham & Asparagus Ring (p. 56)
and allow to cool. Cut in half around the "equator" and remove
the lid. Process the cream until thickened and spoon most of it into
the base, reserving sufficient to decorate. Stud the cream with the
raspberries, reserving a few good ones for decoration. Fit the lid to
the ring and pipe swirls of cream around the top of the ring and
decorate with the raspberries.

PROFITEROLES ✤   *Makes about 20 profiteroles*

1 batch of choux pastry *(p. 105)*
300ml (½ pint) double cream
2 tbsp Cointreau
225g (8 oz) dark chocolate
25g (1 oz) butter
2 tbsp golden syrup
2 tbsp water

Pipe small balls of the pastry onto a greased baking sheet and bake
for 20-30 minutes at 200°C, 400°F, Gas Mark 6. When risen and
golden brown remove and cool on a cake rack. Pierce with a skewer
to allow the steam to escape. Process the cream until thickened,
add the Cointreau and blend with a pulsing action. Pipe or spoon
the cream into the cold profiteroles. Stand a small heat-proof basin
in a pan of boiling water. Put the chocolate, butter, golden syrup
and water into the basin and leave until melted. Stir to blend
thoroughly and pour over the profiteroles just before serving.

RUM BABA ✤   *Makes 12 small ones or 1 large one*

25g (1 oz) fresh yeast *or* **10g (½ oz) dried yeast**
90ml (6 tbsp) tepid milk
75g (3 oz) caster sugar

250g (10 oz) strong plain flour
½ tsp salt
50g (2 oz) softened butter
3 eggs
75g (3 oz) raisins

Syrup:
100g (4 oz) granulated sugar
300ml (½ pint) water
1 tsp lemon juice
2 tbsp rum
1 tbsp honey

Glaze:
6 tbsp apricot jam
4 tbsp water

Decoration:
150ml (¼ pint) whipped cream *(p. 123)*

Blend the yeast, milk and 2 tsp of the sugar in a cup. Leave to stand for 15 minutes until frothy. Put 50g (2 oz) of the flour into the bowl and add the yeast liquid. Process for 30 seconds and leave for 15 minutes until spongy. Add the remaining flour, sugar, salt and butter and eggs and process to blend. Scrape down the sides and process for a further minute. Sprinkle in the raisins and pulse to mix in. Spoon the mixture into a greased ring or funnel spring-form tin (Kugelhopf tin), or into 12 individual brioche or baba moulds. Cover with cling film and leave to prove in a warm place for 40 minutes until the mixture is double in volume. Bake at 200°C, 400°F, Gas Mark 6 for 30 minutes (large) or 10-15 minutes (individual). Cool in the tin for 5 minutes then turn out onto a wire rack. (Freeze at this stage if wished.)

Syrup
Heat together the sugar and water until the sugar is dissolved, then boil until reduced by a quarter. Cool, add the lemon juice, rum and honey. Stand the baba(s) on a lipped plate and spoon the syrup over until soaked in the sponge. Repeat, using the syrup which drains onto the plate until the cake is thoroughly soaked. Transfer the baba(s) to a serving plate.

Glaze

Put the apricot jam and water into the bowl and process until the jam is finely chopped and blended with the water. Heat in a small pan and brush the warm glaze over the baba(s). When cold decorate with the whipped cream.

CHOCOLATE ORANGE CRUNCH ﹌   *Serves 4–6*

225g (8 oz) ginger nut biscuits
50g (2 oz) walnut halves
1 Terry's Plain Chocolate Orange
175g (6 oz) butter
2 eggs
50g (2 oz) caster sugar
50g (2 oz) chopped mixed candied peel

Reduce the biscuits to crumbs (p. 121) and remove from the bowl. Add most of the nuts and process until coarsely chopped. Add to the crumbs. Break the chocolate orange segments into half, cut the butter into smaller lumps. Put both into a heat-proof basin and stand it in a pan of boiling water. Stir the mixture until melted and blended. Put the eggs and sugar into the processor bowl and process until foamy. Add the chocolate mixture, the biscuits, nuts and candied peel. Process until well mixed. Grease a 20cm (8 in) fluted flan ring with removable base and pour in the mixture. Chill in the refrigerator to set. Turn out and decorate with cream and walnuts, if wished.

CHOCOLATE SURPRISE PUDDING ﹌
Serves 4–6

100g (4 oz) self-raising flour
100g (4 oz) soft margarine
100g (4 oz) Barbados sugar
2 tbsp cocoa
2 eggs, beaten

Sauce:
3 tbsp Barbados sugar
3 tbsp cocoa
375ml (¾ pint) boiling water
demerara sugar

Put all the pudding ingredients into the bowl and process until well blended. Spoon into a greased 1 litre (2 pint) ovenproof dish and smooth with the back of the spoon. Blend the sugars and cocoa with a fork and sprinkle over the pudding mixture. Gently pour on the boiling water, in a circular movement. Place the dish on a baking sheet in the oven for 35-40 minutes at 180°C, 350°F, Gas Mark 4. Serve from the dish; don't try to turn out the pudding as the sauce has sunk to the bottom.

PANCAKES

Basic mixtures *(p. 51)*

Pancakes may be cooked in advance, frozen interleaved with greaseproof paper, and re-heated in the oven.

FILLINGS:
Tropical Fruits ✎
Process together the drained contents of a 275g (8 oz) can of pineapple chunks, 2 ripe bananas and 1 tbsp brown sugar, 1 tbsp sultanas and a pinch of mixed spice.

Honeyed Apple ✎
Peel, core and quarter 450g (1 lb) dessert apples and put into the processor bowl with 25g (1 oz) hazelnuts, 2 tbsp of honey. Process until well blended and the nuts are well chopped.

Pastries and Breads

My old school friends will recall the unmanageable stickiness of my pastry, feverishly thrown together in Domestic Science classes. How lucky are the girls (and boys) of today who are also taught the foolproof technique of pastry-making with a food processor. The secret of course is the speed of preparation plus the short handling time which prevents the pastry becoming hard and tough.

If a recipe recommends a quantity of pastry, eg 200g (8 oz), bear in mind that this refers to the quantity of flour used, and not the total weight of the pastry. Fat is best used straight from the refrigerator and cut into 2.5cm (1 in) cubes.

The table below is a guide to the ideal quantities required for different sizes of dish, plate or flan ring. Remember to adjust the fat and liquid quantity proportionately. When making batches for the freezer you should mark on each packet the flour weight for future reference. The quantity you can process in one batch is governed by the capacity of your bowl, so be guided by the manufacturer's instructions.

DISH	PASTRY QUANTITY	SIZE
Shortcrust pastry		
Oval pie dish	*150g (6 oz) covers*	750 ml (1½ pint) dish
	200g (8 oz) covers	1 litre (2 pint) dish
Pie plate	*125g (5 oz) lines OR covers*	18cm (7 in) plate
	150g (6 oz) lines OR covers	22cm (9 in) plate
	200g (8 oz) lines AND covers	18cm (7 in) plate
	250g (10 oz) lines AND covers	22cm (9 in) plate
Tartlets	*200g (8 oz) makes*	18 of 6cm (2½ in) diameter 12 of 8cm (3 in) diameter
Flan ring	*125g (5 oz) lines*	18cm (7 in) ring
	150g (6 oz) lines	20cm (8 in) ring
Puff pastry		
Oval pie dish	*100g (4 oz) covers*	1 litre (2 pint) dish
Suet pastry		
Pudding basin	*200g (8 oz) lines AND covers*	750ml (1½ pints)
	300g (12 oz) lines AND covers	1.4 litres (2½ pints)
Dumplings	*200g (8 oz) makes*	16 of medium size

Because of the efficiency of blending, you may need less liquid to bind the dry ingredients of a shortcrust pastry, so add this gradually. Shortcrust pastries benefit from 30 minutes "resting" in the refrigerator before use.

FLAN CASES

Apart from pastry you can use some more unusual linings for your flans, sweet and savoury, and the food processor will help with the initial chopping of ingredients, as well as the blending.

BREAD

Anyone who has been overawed by the complications of bread making can now bake the most delicious rolls, loaves and yeasted breads. A food processor can only manage a relatively small amount of dough in one batch, compared with the traditional kneading method; however, for many people it is still quicker to make up three batches in the processor. Most manufacturers recommend a maximum mixture using 450g (1 lb) flour, and some manufacturers recommend resting the processor for an hour or two after 5 consecutive operations.

Yeast can be bought either as compressed fresh yeast from health food shops, some chemists and bakers. It will keep for up to 2 weeks in the refrigerator in a small plastic box, or loosely wrapped in a polythene bag. It may also be frozen for up to 6 weeks, divided into usable portions and well wrapped. Blend the frozen yeast straight into the warm liquid or thaw for 20 minutes before use.

Dried yeast keeps for up to a year while sealed. Once opened store it in a *small* airtight container and use within 4 months; so buy in small amounts to ensure freshness.

Blend fresh yeast with hand-hot liquid (38°C/100°F). Don't cream the yeast with the sugar or the bread will taste unpleasantly yeasty. Dried yeast is reconstituted by stirring it with a little sugar into hand-hot liquid, leaving it for 10 minutes in a warm place until the yeast has dissolved and the mixture froths. If there is no froth, the yeast is stale and should not be used.

Bread can be made with white, wheatmeal or wholewheat (granary) flour. Best results are obtained with strong flours which are high in gluten-forming proteins.

Rising time will vary depending on the temperature of the room:

1 hour in a warm place not above 32°C (90°F)
1½-2 hours at room temperature 18-21°C (65-70°F)
4 hours in a cool place.

SHORTCRUST PASTRY 🥄

200g (8 oz) plain flour
large pinch of salt
50g (2 oz) margarine, cut into chunks
50g (2 oz) lard, cut into chunks
3 tbsp cold water

Put the flour, salt and fats into the bowl and process for a few seconds until the mixture resembles breadcrumbs. Take care not to over-process at this point. Remove the pusher and, with the machine running, pour the cold water a spoonful at a time, through the filling tube. Process for 15-20 seconds until a dough is formed in one ball. Wrap the ball in foil and leave in the refrigerator to rest for 30 minutes.

SPICY SHORTCRUST PASTRY

A good pinch of cinnamon added to the flour in the above recipe gives a spicy pastry ideal for mincepies and apple tarts.

SAVOURY SHORTCRUST PASTRY

Add 50g (2 oz) grated Parmesan cheese and a generous amount of freshly-ground black pepper to the flour for a savoury pastry for flans, savoury pies and sausage rolls.

SWEET SHORTCRUST PASTRY ✎

150g (6 oz) plain flour
large pinch of salt
50g (2 oz) caster sugar
75g (3 oz) butter
1 egg

Put the flour, salt, sugar and butter into the bowl and process until it resembles fine breadcrumbs. Break the egg into a small bowl and beat with a fork. With the machine running pour the egg through the feed tube and process briefly until a dough ball is formed. Rest the pastry, wrapped, in the refrigerator for 30 minutes.

WHOLEWHEAT PASTRY ✎

350g (12 oz) wholewheat flour
125g (5 oz) butter or margarine
pinch of salt
1 egg, beaten
a little cold water

Put the flour, butter and salt into the bowl and process until it resembles fine breadcrumbs. Add the egg and process for 5 seconds. Pour in through the filling tube, with the motor running, sufficient cold water to form a dough ball. Add the water a spoonful at a time. Wrap the ball of pastry in foil and refrigerate for half an hour before use.

SUET PASTRY 🍴

200g (8 oz) self-raising flour
1 tsp salt
75g (3 oz) shredded suet
125ml (¼ pint) water, approximately

Put the flour, salt and suet into the bowl and process by pulsing for a couple of seconds. Gradually pour the water through the feed tube with the motor running, until a dough ball forms. Don't over-process.

Dumplings added to a stew or cooked in stock take about 25 minutes. As a tasty alternative use half and half self-raising flour with wholemeal flour and a teaspoon of baking powder. A teaspoon of herbs added to the flour enhances the taste of the crust or dumplings.

HOT WATER CRUST PASTRY 🍴

300g (12 oz) plain flour
1 tsp salt
100g (4 oz) lard
125ml (¼ pint) water

Put the flour and salt into the bowl. Heat the lard and water in a saucepan until the fat melts. Bring to the boil, remove from the heat and add to the flour. Process until it forms a soft paste. This pastry must be used while it is still warm, as it cracks when it cools. Have your other ingredients ready-prepared and if necessary keep the pastry warm, wrapped in polythene, and leave in a warm place.

This quantity makes sufficient for

SIZE	FILLINGS
15cm (6 in) diameter pie	600-700g (1½-1¾ lb) coarsely chopped meat
Small loaf tin shape	450-500g (1-1¼ lb) chopped meat
4 × 8cm (3 in) diameter pies	600g (1½ lb) coarsely chopped meat

CHOUX PASTRY

75g (3 oz) plain flour
50g (2 oz) butter
125ml (¼ pint) water
2 eggs, beaten

Put the flour into the processor bowl. In a small saucepan melt the butter in the water and bring to the boil. Remove from the heat and pour into the bowl and process until it forms a pastry ball. Scrape the sides if necessary. Add half of the egg mixture and blend with short pulsing action until combined, then add the remaining egg. The final pastry should be glossy and of a piping or spooning consistency.

For best results choux pastry should be cooked at 200°C, 400°F, Gas Mark 6. Freeze the pastry after baking and when thawed re-crisp briefly in the oven. Don't add the filling too far in advance or the pastry will become soggy. The above quantity gives approximately:

10 of 10cm (4 in) long eclairs
25 of 4cm (1½ in) long eclairs
10 of 5cm (2 in) diameter choux buns
20 of 3cm (1¼ in) diameter profiteroles.

SAVOURY CHOUX PASTRY

Add to the above recipe with the flour, a pinch of cayenne pepper, ½ tsp mustard powder and 10g (½ oz) grated cheese, for a tasty pastry which can be cooked in profiterole shapes and filled with cream cheese.

BISCUIT CRUMB CASE 🕭

450g (1 lb) plain digestive biscuits, halved
75g (3 oz) caster sugar
100g (4 oz) melted butter

Feed the biscuits through the feed tube with the motor running. Process until they resemble fine breadcrumbs. Add the sugar and pulse to mix in. With the motor running pour the melted butter through the feed tube to form a soft paste. Press into an 18cm (7 in) flan dish and refrigerate.

Variations:
Instead of digestive biscuits use gingernut, chocolate digestive or cookie type biscuits, or breakfast muesli, and if wished add chopped nuts such as walnut, hazelnut, almond or brazil.

OATFLAKE CASE (Sweet or savoury) 🕭

150g (6 oz) margarine, melted
200g (8 oz) oatflakes
and (sweet version) **100g (4 oz) brown sugar**
or (savoury version) **salt and black pepper**

Put all the ingredients into the bowl and process with a pulsing action until well blended. Press into an 18cm (7 in) flan dish and bake for 25 minutes at 190°C, 375°F, Gas Mark 5.

Variation:
Add a good pinch of herbs to the savoury version or a good pinch of mixed spice to the sweet version.

BREADCRUMB CASE (Sweet or savoury) 🕭

225g (8 oz) fresh breadcrumbs *(p. 121)*
150g (6 oz) melted butter
and (sweet version) **50g (2 oz) caster sugar**
or (savoury version) **a pinch of mace**
with salt and peppper

Make the breadcrumbs, if necessary, then add the sugar *or* seasoning, plus the butter. Process with a pulsing action to blend. Press into an 18cm (7 in) flan dish and bake at 190°C, 375°F, Gas Mark 5, for 20-30 minutes.

WHITE BREAD ✍

Makes 1 large loaf or 2 small loaves or 12 rolls

400g (1 lb) strong white flour
10ml (2 tsp) salt
10g ($\frac{1}{2}$ oz) lard
10g ($\frac{1}{2}$ oz) fresh yeast (or 2 tsp dried yeast with 1 tsp caster sugar)
250ml ($\frac{1}{2}$ pint) tepid water

Put the flour, salt and lard into the bowl and process until well mixed. Blend the fresh yeast with half of the water or, if using dried yeast, sprinkle the sugar into half the water, sprinkle in the dried yeast and leave for 10-15 minutes in a warm place to become frothy. Then pour either type of yeast liquid into the bowl and process for a couple of seconds. Add the remaining water, a little at a time, through the filling tube until all the flour is combined. You may not need all of the water. Process for about 1 minute until the dough is no longer sticky. Either leave in the bowl for 1$\frac{1}{2}$ hours to rise in a warm place, or transfer to an oiled polythene bag. When doubled in size return to the bowl and process for about 10 seconds to "knock back". Now decide how to use the dough.

Loaves: Shape the dough and place in a large loaf tin. Leave to prove for about 45 minutes and when doubled in size bake at 230°C, 450°F, Gas Mark 8 for 25 minutes. It is cooked when the base of the loaf sounds hollow when tapped. Variation: add 1 tsp mixed herbs when knocking back to make a delicious herb bread.

Rolls: Weigh the dough and divide into 12 equal portions (roughly 50g/2 oz each). Using the cupped palm of the hand roll each piece on the clean work top to form a roll shape. Place on a greased baking tray, leaving space between each. Cover with polythene and leave in a warm place for about $\frac{1}{2}$ hour to rise. Brush the tops of the rolls with salted water and, if wished, sprinkle with sesame or poppy seeds. Bake for 20 minutes at the top of a hot oven (230°C, 450°F, Gas Mark 8).

GRANARY BREAD &

Makes as above

10g (½ oz) fresh yeast
OR **2 tsp dried yeast with 1 tsp caster sugar**
250ml (½ pint) tepid water
400g (1 lb) granary flour
2 tsp salt
10g (½ oz) lard
1 tsp black treacle

Blend the yeast with the water. If using dried yeast and sugar, blend with the water and allow to stand for 10 minutes until frothy. Process the flour, salt and lard to resemble fine breadcrumbs. Stir the treacle into the yeast liquid until well blended. With the motor running, gradually pour all the yeast liquid through the feed tube onto the flour. Process for 1 minute, transfer to an oiled bowl or polythene bag. Leave to rise until doubled in size. Return to the processor and process for 30 seconds to knock back. With floured hands mould into a rounded cob shape and place in a 20cm (8 in) greased cake tin. Cover with oiled polythene and leave in a warm place to prove (see times for loaves and rolls in above recipe). When risen bake for 35 minutes for a large loaf or 25 minutes for the rolls at 230°C, 450°F, Gas Mark 8.

BRIOCHE &

Batter:

2 tsp dried yeast or 10g (½ oz) fresh yeast
3 tbsp hand-hot milk
1 tsp sugar
25g (1 oz) strong white flour

Other ingredients:

200g (8 oz) strong white flour
large pinch of salt
50g (2 oz) butter
2 eggs, beaten
beaten egg for glazing

Batter

Stir the yeast into the milk. If using dried yeast also add the sugar and leave to stand for 10 minutes. Stir in the flour and leave in a warm place for about 20 minutes until frothy.

Method

Put the flour, salt and sugar (if not already used) into the processor bowl and process briefly to mix. Add the butter and process briefly to form breadcrumbs. Add the beaten eggs to the frothy batter and with the motor running pour the liquid through the feed tube and process for a minute to form a soft dough. Cover and leave to rise until doubled in size. Return to the bowl and process briefly to knock back. Either grease 12 individual brioche tins or 12 deep bun tins. Divide the dough equally between the tins. Cut a quarter from each piece and form the larger piece into a ball and place in the tin. Use your index finger to press a hole in the centre of the ball, and place the remaining small piece, rolled into a ball, on top. Glaze with beaten egg, cover and leave to prove for about 30 minutes until light and puffy. Bake for about 20 minutes at 230°C, 450°F, Gas Mark 8 until golden brown.

Variation: Cut a 225g (8 oz) pack of frankfurter sausages into 1cm (½ in) chunks, and press into the finger hole before adding the "lid". It makes very upmarket sausage rolls.

DANISH ORANGE RING &

15g (½ oz) fresh yeast
OR
2 tsp dried yeast with ½ tsp caster sugar
5 tbsp tepid milk
225g (8 oz) plain flour
pinch of salt
1 egg, beaten
25g (1 oz) butter, melted
50g (2 oz) brown sugar
50g (2 oz) sultanas
1 orange
pinch of cinnamon
100g (4 oz) icing sugar
glacé cherries
angelica to decorate

If using dried yeast put it into the bowl with the sugar, milk and 50g (2 oz) of the flour. Process until blended and allow to stand for 25 minutes until frothy. If using fresh yeast, put it into the bowl with the milk and the 50g (2 oz) of flour. Process to blend. In both cases then add the egg, half the butter and the salt, and process to blend. Add the remaining flour and process for 2 minutes. Either leave in the bowl or transfer to an oiled bowl or polythene bag and leave in a warm place until doubled in size. Then roll out to form a rectangle 30 × 23cm (12 × 9 in). Brush with the remaining butter and sprinkle with the brown sugar and sultanas. Remove and chop the zest of the orange (see p. 125). Sprinkle over the pastry with the cinnamon. Roll up like a Swiss roll, but from the longer edge. Seal the two ends together, forming a ring. Stand on a greased baking sheet and use kitchen scissors to snip wide slashes 2.5cm (1 in) apart, around the top of the ring. Cover with oiled polythene and leave to prove in a warm place for 30 minutes. Bake for 30-35 minutes in a moderate oven (190°C, 375°F, Gas Mark 5). Cool on a wire tray.

To decorate, place the icing sugar into the clean bowl and through the feed tube add 1 tsp cold water. Process to blend and if necessary add a second tsp of water, to give a coating consistency. Spoon the icing over the cooled ring and decorate with glacé cherries and angelica. Serve when set. If wished, freeze before icing.

Cakes, Scones and Biscuits

Cake making with a food processor is faster and less strenuous than the arm-aching wooden spoon method; but do not expect the same lighter-than-air sponges which can only be created by beating in air either by hand or using a food mixer. Most food processors cannot incorporate the same amount of air and instead the all-in-one method (Victoria Sandwich, below) uses baking powder as well as self-raising flour to achieve the extra rise.

If you have a food processor capable of whisking egg whites, you will be able to produce the traditional type of sponges by following the manufacturer's instructions. When converting your own recipes, take care when adding the liquid as you may require slightly less when using your food processor.

When mixing, do so in short bursts, periodically scraping down mixture from the sides. Always add dried fruit, glacé cherries and chocolate chips last of all, using a pulsing action, otherwise the steel blade will chop them out of recognition.

Use your food processor to make marzipan and icing to decorate the cakes.

VICTORIA SANDWICH CAKE ✑

100g (4 oz) self-raising flour
1 tsp baking powder
100g (4 oz) soft margarine
100g (4 oz) caster sugar
2 eggs, beaten

Grease and line 2 × 18cm (7 in) sandwich tins. Put the flour and baking powder into the bowl and pulse to mix. Add all the remaining ingredients and process until smooth and glossy. Spread into the prepared tins and bake for about 30 minutes at 190°C, 375°F, Gas Mark 5. When cool turn out onto a wire rack, fill with jam and dredge the top with caster sugar.

Variation; Add 2 tbsp golden syrup and 2 tbsp cocoa powder mixed to a paste with 2 tbsp warm water.

CUP CAKES   *Makes 18*

1 batch of Victoria Sandwich mixture *(above)*
Butter cream icing *(p. 124)*
Glacé cherries

Stand paper baking cases on a baking sheet. Spoon the cake mixture into the cases, filling about two thirds full. Bake at 190°C, 375°F, Gas Mark 5 for 15-18 minutes. Cool and decorate with butter cream icing, topped with a glacé cherry.

Variations:
Butterfly Cakes – use a sharp knife to slice the domed top from each of the cakes and cut in half to form 'wings'. Pipe butter cream on top of each cake and arrange the two halves as wings.

Chocolate Chip Cakes – add 50g (2 oz) chocolate chips to the basic mixture and pulse to mix in.

COFFEE & WALNUT CAKE ✑

Make a batch of Victoria Sandwich Cake (above), adding 1 tsp of coffee essence and 25g (1 oz) chopped walnuts.

Coffee icing:
200g (7 oz) icing sugar
40g (1½ oz) butter
2 tbsp water
25g (1 oz) caster sugar
2 tsp coffee essence

Put the icing sugar into the bowl. Put the butter, water, caster sugar and coffee essence into a saucepan and stir until the butter melts and the sugar dissolves. Don't allow to boil. Pour onto the icing sugar and process until a soft fudge icing is produced, scraping down the sides if necessary. Use half the icing to sandwich the cake together and then top with the remainder.

TIPPLE CAKE ✎

150ml (¼ pint) light ale
175g (6 oz) demerara sugar
125g (4 oz) margarine
275g (10 oz) mixed dried fruit
350g (12 oz) self-raising flour
1 tsp baking powder
2 tsp mixed spice
1 egg, beaten

Put the beer, sugar, margarine and dried fruit into a saucepan. Bring to the boil, reduce the heat and simmer for 10 minutes. Remove from the heat, pour into the bowl and cool. Grease and line a 20cm (8 in) cake tin. When the liquid is cold add all the remaining ingredients and process until well blended. Pour into the cake tin and bake for 1½ hours at 180°C, 350°F, Gas Mark 4. Turn out and cool on a cooling rack.

GINGERBREAD ✎

100g (4 oz) margarine
150g (6 oz) black treacle
50g (2 oz) golden syrup
125ml (¼ pint) milk
2 eggs, beaten
200g (8 oz) plain flour

1 tbsp ground ginger
1 tsp bicarbonate of soda
1 tsp mixed spice
50g (2 oz) caster sugar
50g (2 oz) sultanas

Grease and line a large loaf tin. Put the margarine, treacle and golden syrup into a medium saucepan and warm together, but don't allow to boil. Remove from the heat, stir in the milk and allow to cool. Put the flour, ginger, bicarbonate of soda, mixed spice and sugar into the bowl and pulse to blend. Add the cooled liquid and eggs, and process until completely blended. Add the sultanas and pulse to mix. Turn into the loaf tin and bake at 150°C, 300°F, Gas Mark 2 for 1¼ hours. Cool in the tin for 10 minutes before turning out onto a cooling rack.

CARROT CAKE 🥄 🥄

225g (8 oz) carrots
100g (4 oz) walnuts
175ml (6 fl oz) corn oil
150g (6 oz) caster sugar
3 eggs
1 tsp vanilla essence
150g (6 oz) self-raising flour
1 tsp baking powder
1 tsp cinnamon
1 tsp salt

Icing:
85g (3 oz) cream cheese
50g (2 oz) butter
few drops of vanilla flavouring
100g (4 oz) icing sugar
8 walnut halves

Grease and line a 20cm (8 in) cake tin. Use the shredding disc to grate the peeled carrots. Remove from the bowl and fit the steel blade. Use to coarsely chop the walnuts. Add all the remaining cake ingredients to the bowl and process until well blended. Add the carrot and mix in with a pulsing action. Turn into the cake tin and bake at 180°C, 350°F, Gas Mark 4 for approximately 1¼ hours. The cake should spring back when pressed. Cool in the tin for 5 minutes before turning out onto a cooling rack. To make the icing put all the ingredients except the walnuts into the clean bowl and process until smooth. Spread over the top and sides of the cold cake and decorate with the walnut halves.

DATE LOAF ⇗

100g (4 oz) stoned dates
200g (8 oz) self-raising flour
½ tsp salt
2 tsp mixed spice
100g (4 oz) butter
100g (4 oz) caster sugar
1 egg plus sufficient milk to make 125ml (¼ pint) liquid

Chill the dates then put into the bowl with 1 tbsp of flour taken from the specified amount. Chop the dates and add the remaining flour, salt and mixed spice. Add the butter, cut into cubes, and process briefly to form breadcrumbs. Add the sugar and mix in with a pulsing action. Beat the egg with the milk and add to the mixture through the feed tube with the motor running. Turn into a greased and lined large loaf tin and bake at 180°C, 350°F or Gas Mark 4 for about 1¼ hours. Cool in the tin before turning out.

BANANA TEABREAD ⇗

50g (2 oz) walnuts
2 large ripe bananas
200g (8 oz) self-raising flour
½ tsp salt
100g (4 oz) softened butter
150g (6 oz) caster sugar
100g (4 oz) sultanas
2 eggs, beaten

Put the walnuts into the bowl and process until coarsely chopped. Peel the bananas, break each into 4 pieces and process with the walnuts until mashed. Add all the remaining ingredients and process until well mixed. Spoon the mixture into a large greased and lined loaf tin. Smooth the surface and bake for 1-1¼ hours at 180°C, 350°F, Gas Mark 4. Cool in the loaf tin for 15 minutes then turn out onto a cooling rack. When cold, slice and serve spread with butter.

MARMALADE LOAF 🥄

2 tea bags
300ml (½ pint) boiling water
450g (1 lb) mixed dried fruit
1 orange
150g (6 oz) brown sugar
4 tbsp thick cut marmalade
1 egg, beaten
350g (12 oz) self-raising flour
2 tsp baking powder
1 tsp mixed spice

The day before, put the tea bags in the boiling water and leave there until the tea is cold. Remove the bags and put the dried fruit into the tea. Leave to soak overnight. Next day finely chop the zest of the orange (see p. 125) and squeeze the juice. Put the flour and remaining ingredients into the bowl, add the chopped zest and orange juice and the strained tea. Reserve the fruit. Process the mixture until well blended, add the dried fruit and mix in with a pulsing action. Grease and line a large loaf tin and bake for 1¾ hours until golden brown, at 180°C, 350°F, Gas Mark 4.

POTATO CAKES 🥄 🥄

450g (1 lb) potatoes, peeled and boiled
½ tsp salt
75g (3 oz) soft margarine
125g (4 oz) plain flour
75g (3 oz) raisins *(optional)*

Use the grating disc to grate the cold potato. Remove the disc and the potato. Fit the steel blade, add the flour, salt and margarine and the grated potato and process until a dough is formed. Add the raisins, if wished, and pulse to mix. Press evenly over a greased baking sheet and bake at 220°C, 425°F, Gas Mark 7 for 30-40 minutes until lightly browned. Cut into squares and serve hot.

Variation: Omit the raisins and serve hot spread with butter and sprinkled with sugar.

SCONES &

200g (8 oz) self-raising flour
½ tsp salt
50g (2 oz) butter or margarine
25g (1 oz) caster sugar
125ml (¼ pint) milk
beaten egg to glaze

Put the flour and salt into the bowl and add the fat, cut into cubes. Process briefly to form breadcrumbs. Add the sugar and mix in with a pulsing action. Add the milk through the feed tube with the motor running, adding sufficient to produce a ball of dough. Roll out about 1cm (½ in) thick and cut into 10-12 rounds using a 5cm (2 in) cutter. Place on a baking tray and glaze with beaten egg. Bake for 8-10 minutes at 220°C, 425°F, Gas Mark 7. Serve warm or cold, split and spread with butter and jam.

Variations:
Omit sugar and substitute 50g (2 oz) grated cheese, or add 25g (1 oz) sultanas and 25g (1 oz) chopped nuts with the sugar.

DROP SCONES &

100g (4 oz) plain flour
pinch of salt
1 tsp bicarbonate of soda
1½ tsp cream of tartar
1 tbsp caster sugar
1 egg
1 tsp golden syrup
6 tbsp milk

Put all the ingredients into the bowl and process until a smooth batter is produced. Heat a heavy, thick based frypan, lightly oiled.

When very hot, drop dessertspoonfuls of the mixture onto the pan, leaving space for them to spread. When bubbles burst through the surface, about 2-3 minutes, turn over with a pallet knife and cook the other side for a minute. Keep warm wrapped in a clean teatowel while the remainder is cooked. Serve warm, spread with butter.

CHOCOLATE OATMEAL COOKIES 🍪

Makes about 36

100g (4 oz) softened butter
100g (4 oz) caster sugar
75g (3 oz) plain flour
pinch of salt
1 egg
1 tsp vanilla essence
25g (1 oz) rolled oats
100g (4 oz) chocolate chips

Put the butter and sugar into the bowl and process until creamed. Add all the remaining ingredients except the chocolate and process until well blended. Add the chocolate chips and mix in with a pulsing action. Drop rounded teaspoons of the mixture onto greased baking sheets. You may need to cook in batches. Bake for 12-15 minutes at 180°C, 350°F, Gas Mark 4, until lightly browned. Cool for a while on the baking sheet before transferring to a wire tray.

VIENNA SHORTCAKES 🍪

Makes 6

75g (3 oz) plain flour
25g (1 oz) cornflour
100g (4 oz) softened butter
40g (1½ oz) icing sugar
few drops of almond essence

Topping:
Icing sugar and raspberry jam

Put the biscuit ingredients into the bowl and process until well blended. Spoon the mixture into a piping bag fitted with a large rosette nozzle. Stand 6 paper baking cases on a baking sheet. Pipe the mixture into the cases, piping twice around the edge of each

case to form a hollow in the centre. Bake for about 20 minutes until
risen and pale, at 180°C, 350°F, Gas Mark 4. Cool, dust with icing
sugar and spoon a little raspberry jam into the centre of each cake.

SHORTBREAD 🍧

Makes 12 pieces

200g (8 oz) butter
100g (4 oz) caster sugar
250g (10 oz) plain flour
50g (2 oz) semolina

Cream the butter and sugar until light and creamy. Add the flour
and semolina and blend well until it forms a paste. Divide the
mixture between two greased 18cm (7 in) sandwich tins. Use the
back of a spoon to press the mixture evenly over the surface of the
tin. Use the back of a knife gently to score the surface into 6 equal
segments in each tin. Bake in the oven at 160°C, 325°F, Gas Mark
3, for 40 minutes or until golden brown. Cool before turning out
onto a cooling rack. Either split into 12 pieces when thoroughly
cold or use to make strawberry shortbread (p. 90).

GINGER NUTS 🍧

Makes 24

75g (3 oz) butter
50g (2 oz) caster sugar
2 tbsp golden syrup
225g (8 oz) plain flour
1 tsp baking powder
2 tsp ground ginger

Put the butter, sugar and syrup into a small pan and heat, stirring
continuously until the butter is melted and the sugar dissolved. Do
not boil. Put the remaining ingredients into the bowl and pour the
melted ingredients over. Process until a soft dough is formed.
Divide the mixture into 24 small pieces. Roll each into a ball then
place them on a greased baking sheet, with plenty of space between.
Flatten each ball with the sugared base of a glass. Bake for 10-15
minutes at 180°C, 350°F, Gas Mark 4. Cool slightly on the baking
sheet before transferring to a wire tray.

NUTTY CHOCS &

Makes about 15

25g (1 oz) hazelnuts
250g (8 oz) plain flour
125g (4 oz) caster sugar
125g (4 oz) soft margarine
1 egg, beaten
1 tsp vanilla essence
25g (1 oz) chocolate chips

Put the hazelnuts into the bowl and process until coarsely chopped. Add all the remaining ingredients except the chocolate chips and process until a soft dough is formed. Add the chocolate and process with a pulsing action to mix. Shape into a long roll 3.5cm (1½ in) diameter. Wrap in foil and chill in the refrigerator for about 1 hour. Slice the biscuit roll into discs 5mm (¼ in) thick and place on a greased baking sheet. Bake for 7-8 minutes at 200°C, 400°F, Gas Mark 6. Leave on the baking sheet for a couple of minutes before transferring to a wire rack to cool.

PEANUT CRUNCH &

50g (2 oz) salted peanuts
50g (2 oz) plain flour
50g (2 oz) wholemeal flour
75g (3 oz) grated cheese
50g (2 oz) butter
good pinch of salt
good pinch of cayenne pepper

Process the peanuts until coarsely chopped. Remove from the bowl. Put all the remaining ingredients into the bowl and process until well mixed. Press the mixture into a greased baking tin 28 × 18cm (11 × 7 in). Sprinkle the peanuts over the mixture and press into the dough. Bake for 20 minutes at 180°C, 350°F, Gas Mark 4. Cut into squares and allow to cool in the tin.

Miscellaneous

As you become accustomed to your food processor you will discover a number of new uses from time-saving basics such as breadcrumbs, to money-saving cream making. Many of these hints are listed below. There are certain things that you shouldn't try, such as grinding rice, pulses, sugar or coffee beans, as the steel blade will become blunt.

BISCUIT CRUMBS

Halve the biscuits, such as digestives, and drop through the feed tube onto the turning blades.

BREADCRUMBS

Use any type of bread, sliced or unsliced, with the crusts removed. Break sliced bread into quarters and tear unsliced bread into 2.5cm (1 in) cubes. Fill the bowl no more than half full then process for a few seconds until the breadcrumbs are formed. Store in plastic bags and freeze until required. Keep white and brown breadcrumbs separate for different uses.

BUTTERS 🍴

Unusual butters are delicious as an accompaniment to grilled steaks or spread between thick slices of a French stick and reheated in the oven.

If to be used with steaks, prepare the butter several hours in advance, shape into a roll, wrap in foil and refrigerate for an hour at least. Cut into slices and place on top of the meat just before serving.

Herb 🍴
Process together until well blended 100g (4 oz) butter, 2 tbsp dried mixed herbs.

Garlic 🍴
Put two peeled garlic cloves into the bowl and process until finely chopped. Add 100g (4 oz) butter and process until well blended.

Parsley 🍴
Process the parsley until well chopped (see Herbs) and add 100g (4 oz) butter and the juice of ½ lemon. Process until well blended.

Anchovy 🍴
Drain the fillets from a 50g (2 oz) can of anchovies and process with 100g (4 oz) butter and 1 tsp lemon juice.

CHEESE 🍴 🍴

Grating
Hard cheese should be cut into 2.5cm (1 in) cubes and processed using the steel blade for 20-30 seconds until finely chopped.

Softer (but not cream) cheeses should be grated using the grating disc. Quantities of the grated cheese may be bagged and sealed and kept for a few days in the refrigerator or frozen. Use straight from the freezer for sauces and general cooking.

Slicing 🍴
Use the slicing disc with firm cheese and trim the cheese to fit the feed tube.

CHOCOLATE &

Chill the chocolate then break into small, even chunks. Put into the cold bowl and process with the steel blade until finely chopped.

CREAM MAKING &

Keep unsalted butter in the refrigerator and you have the basis of stand-by cream at any time, and at half the price. Although slightly heavier than fresh cream this will not be apparent if combined with chopped zest of lemon or other fruit (see page 125). You must use unsalted butter to make this cream. Chill the made cream well before whipping and take care not to over-whip – it is best to use a hand whisk. Use soon after whipping and use any of these creams within 2 days of making. When flavouring with chocolate use grated chocolate rather than melted chocolate which causes this home-made cream to curdle. Don't try to freeze this cream.

Pouring cream: 75g (3 oz) unsalted butter, 100ml (4 fl oz) milk
Whipping cream: 100g (4 oz) unsalted butter, 100ml (4 fl oz) milk
Double cream: 125g (5 oz) unsalted butter, 100ml (4 fl oz milk)

Cut the butter into small pieces about 1cm (½ in) cube and heat with the milk until melted. Do not boil. Pour into the bowl and process with three 10 second pulses. Pour into a bowl or jug and refrigerate for at least 2 hours, preferably overnight for whipping cream.

CREAM, WHIPPING &

Bought (as opposed to home-made) double cream may be whipped using the steel blade, but the result will not be as stiff as cream whipped with a beater. Chill the cream before whipping and use a minimum of 300ml (½ pint).

CRISPS &

Use the slicing disc to slice potatoes very thinly. Wash well in cold water, drain on a cloth and pat dry. Deep fry in hot fat, a small quantity at a time. When golden brown remove, drain on kitchen paper, season with salt and serve warm or cold.

DRIED FRUITS ❧

To chop dried fruits such as apricots, prunes (stoned), glacé cherries, dates, etc, first chill them for about 1 hour. Process with a little of the flour taken from the recipe.

HERBS ❧

Wash fresh herbs and dry between kitchen paper. Remove stems and process for 5-10 seconds using the steel blade.

ICINGS ❧

Almond Paste
Sufficient to cover the top and sides of a 23cm (9 in) round or 20cm (8 in) square cake.

150g (6 oz) icing sugar
150g (6 oz) caster sugar
300g (12 oz) ground almonds
4 egg yolks
3 tbsp lemon juice
3 drops of almond essence

Put all the ingredients into the bowl and process until a smooth paste is formed.

Butter Cream Icing ❧

Sufficient to fill or decorate an 18cm (7 in) cake

50g (2 oz) softened butter
100g (4 oz) icing sugar
2-3 drops of flavouring

Put the cubed butter into the bowl, add the icing sugar and the flavouring and process until completely blended, scraping down the sides as necessary.

Variations:
Lemon – add the grated rind of 1 lemon (see Zest) and 1 tbsp lemon juice.
Mocha – add 1 tsp of cocoa powder and 1 tsp coffee essence.

Glacé Icing ✌

100g (4 oz) icing sugar
1 tbsp water

Put into the bowl and process until completely blended.

Creamy Orange Filling ✌

1 orange
75g (3 oz) caster sugar
200g (7 oz) cream cheese

Finely chop the zest of the orange (see below). Add the sugar, cream cheese and the juice of half the orange. Process until it forms a thick cream.

LEMON CURD ✌   *Makes approx. 1kg (2 lb)*

4 lemons
100g (4 oz) melted butter
450g (1 lb) caster sugar
4 eggs

Finely chop the zest of the four lemons (see below). Squeeze the juice of *two* of the lemons and add to the zest with all the remaining ingredients. Process until well blended. Pour into a 1 litre (2 pint) basin. Stand in a large saucepan of simmering water and stir continuously until the sugar is dissolved and the mixture thickens. Remove the basin from the pan, allow to cool, cover and store in the refrigerator for up to 3 weeks.

NUTS

Nuts may be chopped coarsely or finely as wished by processing for 10-20 seconds with the steel blade.

ZEST OF LEMON OR ORANGE ✌

Use a sharp potato peeler to remove the zest of the fruit. Take care only to remove the coloured part and not the bitter white pith. Put the strips into the bowl and process with part of the sugar taken from a sweet recipe, or alone if to be used in a savoury recipe.

Index